Psychic Perception :
The Magic of Extrasensory Power

BOOKS BY
DR. JOSEPH MURPHY

Psychic Perception: The Magic of Extrasensory Power

Joseph Murphy, D.D., D.R.S., Ph.D., LL.D.

 DEVORSS *Publications*

First DeVorss Edition, 1996
ISBN 0-87516-670-9
Library of Congress Card Catalog No.: 71-150580

DeVorss & Company, Publisher
P.O. Box 550
Marina del Rey, CA 90294

Printed in The United States of America

What This Book Can Do for You

Everyone possesses psychic power, and can be presently aware of events and experiences transcending the five senses. You can easily learn to use these extraordinary psychic powers to benefit your daily living to an extent that will amaze you.

Vast numbers of people in all walks of life are constantly dealing with such powers as clairvoyance, whereby one perceives things and situations at a distance; precognition, which is the ability to see future events as happening now in one's mind; telepathy, where one communicates mentally with others, collapsing time and space limitations; and retrocognition, which is the ability to see events in the past. All of these powers are latent in all of us.

You will read in this book how a great many people, by using extrasensory or psychic perception, saved the lives of loved ones, how they prevented accidents or financial disasters to themselves, and much more of vital significance in complex daily living.

Why You Need This Book

This book teaches you how to meet and overcome the challenges, difficulties, trials, and other problems of daily living. It explains how to contact the Infinite Healing Presence within you, and supplies you with specific techniques for putting your extrasensory powers into operation at once for your practical benefit.

It is for the express purpose of teaching you, the reader, how to align and use these extraordinary and perceptive psychic powers in your daily life that I wrote this book. I have endeavored on every page to explain extrasensory perception and healing; premonitions; how dreams avert tragedies; clairaudience; how dreams have brought fortunes into the lives of people; precognition; techniques for eradicating negative predictions; astral travel; psychic perception; and the law of plenty in all its aspects, including the financial ones.

What Psychic Perception Has Done for Others

I have taught and written about dreams, clairvoyance, out-of-the-body experiences, and other miracle-working powers of the mind for over 30 years, here and abroad. All my life I have had psychic experiences and have perceived events long before they happened, in some instances 20 years before. I have witnessed and heard of the following tremendous changes in the lives of countless numbers of people who sincerely used their extrasensory powers:

- Wealth bestowed in avalanches of abundance
- Discoveries of hidden treasure
- Psychic healing of maladies thought incurable
- Locating long-lost friends and relatives
- Specific and valuable benefits of astral travel and out-of-the-body experiences
- Lives saved through psychic impressions of impending danger
- Public acclaim, honor, and recognition
- Dreams revealing amazing answers to daily problems
- Happier marriages and more zestful daily living

— New ideas for sales programs, sound business development

— The prevention of many unnecessary tragedies

— And, above all, the joyous satisfaction of the answered desire for psychic awareness in handling the problems of daily living, in all its ramifications, successfully.

Psychic Perception Operates in All Walks of Life and at All Levels

According to my observations and experience, the men, women, and teenagers who use extrasensory perception in their daily lives come from every level of society and from every possible income bracket. They are taxi drivers, housewives, stenographers, doctors, students, college professors, motion picture stars, chiropractors, pharmacists, space scientists, and truck drivers—to name just a few of those who have found perceptive awareness of their psychic abilities to benefit them daily in a real and concrete way. These people have discovered the wonders of disciplined imagination; banished their sense of loneliness and harmful obsessions; established the mental equivalent of a million dollars in their subconscious mind; through previsions of impending tragedies for themselves and others were able to avoid them; solved legal problems; gained freedom from the fear of so-called voodoo or evil eye or psychic attack and achieved peace of mind and confidence to handle any situation for a great new life.

Unique Features of This Book

The unique features of this book are its down-to-earth practicality and everyday utility. You will learn to use your inborn extraordinary ability to visualize future events, and, if they are indicated to be negative, change them through scientific prayer. You will learn how to develop your intuition and other psychic powers which will set you on the fast

high road to happiness, peace of mind, and freedom from
limitation of any sort.

How the Infinite Healing Presence
Answers You in Dreams and
Visions of the Night

You will read in this book fascinating accounts of out-of-
the-body experiences, sometimes called extrasensory or astral
traveling; clairvoyance; clairaudience; how to make extrasensory perception work for you; how spiritually advanced
individuals can appear and reappear to others at will; communication with loved ones in the spirit world; the pros and
cons of reincarnation and why the author explodes the
popular myths about karma, life cycles, child prodigies,
memories of former lives, inequality at birth, the handicapped, the so-called unfortunate. The chapter on reincarnation will heal you of the age-old taboos, strictures, grievous
bondage and thralldom that shackle you to frustration and
repeated failure.

Let Wonders Happen in Your Life— Beginning Now!

The greatest working truths in life are the simplest. In this
book, I have taken a new look at reincarnation and communication with the so-called dead, and I have presented these
great truths with the maximum of simplicity and dramatic
clarity to help your powers of psychic perception.

This book will show you how to solve your problems of
daily living and receive guidance and the blessings that come
with true awareness. Begin now, today, to let wonders
happen in your life! Keep on using this book until the day
breaks for you with the light of psychic perception—giving
you undisputed dominion over your life the way you want to
live it.

The Author

Table of Contents

11

Subconscious Mind . A Clear-Cut Lead Came into Her
Mind . How Dave Built a Solid Foundation . His Founda-
tion Technique . His Reversed Attitude in Perception
Brought Him Assets of a Quarter of a Million Dollars . His
"Movie" Technique . His Facial Tic Was Ruining His
Career . She Didn't Have to Be Lonely . Points to
Remember

Your Subconscious Reasons Deductively Only . An Inter-
esting Hypnotic Experiment Regarding Past Lives . The
Reason for the Failure . An Experiment with Mr. X's
Sister . Have You Lived Before? . Important Points to
Recall . The Psychological Explanation of Having Been
There Before . Why You May Say, "It Seems I Have
Always Known Him" . Why Is It Possible to Remember
Anything That Has Ever Transpired? . There Is Only One
Being or Life-Principle . Where Did You Come from
Before You Were Born? . Why Is an Innocent Child Born
Deaf, Lame, Blind, or Crippled? . Reincarnation and Time
Cycles . You Are What You Think All Day Long . You
Are Here to Learn the Laws of Life . Why Do Babies and
Young Children Meet with Sickness, Accidents, and
Tragedies? . The Law of Mind Is Good and Very Good
. She Said She Choked People in a Former Life . The
Explanation . Why Some Children Are Born Blind, Deaf,
and Deformed and Others Are Born Healthy . What Is the
Law of Averages? . The Mystery of Child Prodigies
. Look Back at Your Ancestry . A New Beginning Is a
New End . Your Genetic Record . What Is Biological
Atavism? . What Is a Genius? . Why Do Infant Mathe-
matical Prodigies Lose Their Gift? . Some Remarkable
Cases . Realize a Great Truth . Your Storehouse of Mem-
ory . Why Is There Inequality at Birth? . How Some
Look at Justice . You Are Not a Victim of Karma . How
to Accept Your Good Now . Your Time Is Now . The
Author's View of Reincarnation . Points to Remember

1

How to Become Aware
of the Psychic Power of Your Mind

I am writing the first chapter of this book at the beautiful Kona Inn overlooking the ocean on the island of Hawaii. Hundreds of sailboats are to be seen on the ocean; I took a trip on one of the fishing boats yesterday. On the boat was a little boy about 12 years old, who was learning to navigate it. On telling him what I planned to do in the island—namely, write a book on psychic principles—he told me that a month ago when his father died on the island of Oahu, which is a few hundred miles away, he knew it and ran in and told his mother, "Mom, papa is dead. I saw him and talked to him." His father's death was later confirmed by long distance phone.

In the mind-principle, there is no time or space, and when the father was passing over to the next dimension of life, he desired to let his family know it. His son, who was very psychic and receptive, had picked up the father's telepathic message. The little boy also had a clairvoyant vision of his father, who appeared to him and said, "Good-bye."

It should be realized that every person has these psychic capacities. They are more or less dormant, and are often suppressed since they are frequently ridiculed by other members of a family.

You Are Psychic

How often have you thought of a person and then heard the phone ring, and, behold, you knew it was your friend calling; or you may have sensed that someone close to you needed you and when you called on that person you discovered that your intuitive sense was accurate.

Chatting this morning at breakfast, in one of the beautiful Japanese restaurants here, with a man of Japanese parentage born on the Island, I told him I was writing a book on psychic phenomena. He thereupon asked me if I could help a girl who was slowly dying due to her belief that someone in Tahiti had put the "fix" (a native curse) on her. We visited her home and I spent a few hours talking to her, explaining to her that suggestions of others had no power unless she gave the other power, when it would then become auto-suggestion, and that actually she was destroying herself. It began to dawn on her that she was a victim of suggestion and that her only enemy was the fear in her own mind. Job said, *The thing which I greatly feared has come upon me* (Job 3:25).

This girl had been brought up in a convent and had a good religious background. I wrote down the following great truths: *If God be for us, who can be against us?* (Romans 8:31). *No man shall set on thee to hurt thee* (Acts 18:10). *Nothing shall by any means hurt you* (Luke 10:19). *There shall no evil happen to the just* (Proverbs 12:21). *Neither shall any plague come nigh thy dwelling* (Psalm 91:10). *They shall bear thee up in their hands, lest thou dash thy foot against a stone* (Psalm 91:12). *A thousand shall fall at thy side, and ten thousand at thy right hand; but it shall not come nigh thee* (Psalm 91:7).

We recited these truths out loud together, and I suggested to her that whenever fear thoughts came to her mind, she should affirm immediately, "I am alive with the Life of God." The explanation was the cure, and much to the surprise of my Japanese friend, she ate a hearty Thanksgiving lunch with us and joked and laughed gaily. On parting, she said to me, "Never will I doubt again that there is but One Power, and that It moves for good." She is now bubbling over with the joy of life. Psychic perception into the cause of her trouble gave her a new life.

This Thanksgiving morning I had planned to have breakfast in the Kona Inn where I have been staying, but an over-whelming urge came over me to walk up the street until I came to a Japanese restaurant where a big sign said, "Breakfast is now being served." And it was there that I met the man who was seeking to help the above-mentioned girl. He had tried everything in the way of medical and pastoral counseling to no avail; she would not listen to her counselors and doctors, insisting instead that she was doomed to die. He was very depressed because he had planned to marry her.

This was psychic perception at work in my case, the Infinite Intelligence of my subconscious mind acting on me compelling me to go to that particular restaurant and meet this agitated and disturbed soul and answer his problem. This Creative Intelligence brought both of us together in Divine order. Truly, "Man does not know the causes of his actions."

A Thanksgiving Phone Call

This afternoon as I continued writing this chapter, I received a phone call from the island of Maui. This was from an old friend whom I had visited a few days ago as I flew from Kona to Maui. She said that she had exciting news: that a medical doctor whom we had prayed for and who was incapacitated in bed had called her and said, "Something happened to me Tuesday A strange feeling came over me; I felt a healing force flowing through me." Today, my friend says that this doctor is going out to a Thanksgiving lunch and dinner and is perfectly all right.

This was psychic perception at work. In this beautiful home in Maui, where I was a guest, my hostess had said, "Let us pray for a doctor friend of mine who hurt his back so severely he can't work or walk and is lying incapacitated in bed." We joined together, praying as follows: "This doctor is known in Divine Mind, which knows all things. The Infinite Healing Presence which made him knows how to restore him completely. The vitalizing, healing, energizing power of the Infinite One is now flowing through this doctor making him whole and perfect. The river of peace and love saturate his whole being, and the miraculous power of Infinite Life animates and sustains him so that at this moment every atom of his being dances to the rhythm of the Eternal God-Presence within him."

We meditated on these truths for four or five minutes, realizing that the Healing Power was being resurrected within him, and the phone call was the response to our realization of the Infinite Healing Presence. *Say in a word, and my servant shall be healed* (Luke 7:7). This Biblical phrase does not mean you send any healing wave or thought-wave to anybody, but rather that you have a deep, inner feeling, an awareness or conviction that the Healing Love of God is now resurrected in the subconscious of the other person. If you have the realization, the healing will follow. This implies, of course, the receptivity and open-mindedness of the person you are praying for. This is letting psychic perception work for you. *Psyche* means the soul, mind, or spirit; *perception* means awareness of the truth about a person or a situation. It means to inwardly perceive the truth about any problem, whether it pertains to mathematics, navigation, or whatever.

A Dream That Came True

I had a most interesting conversation with a taxi driver,

whose father is Chinese and whose mother is a native Hawaiian. He told me that about five years ago he found that he was saying to himself frequently, "I need more wealth; I need a home for my family." One night he had a vivid dream in which a Chinese sage appeared to him, showed him a certain area of land near the Kona Coast, and instructed him to buy it. He did so, and today it has advanced 15 times in value.

The dream has made him independently wealthy. He was alert and on the *qui vive* through following the lead which came to him from his subliminal depths. He knew nothing about the workings of his subconscious mind, but the law worked for him because he was quietly and feelingly saying to himself, "I need more money, I need a new home, and somehow the answer will come." He was not aware of the powers of his deeper mind; nevertheless, it responded in the form of a dream, which he had the mental ability to interpret accurately, and he acted accordingly. The Bible says, *I, the Lord,* (law of your subconscious mind) *will make myself known unto him in a vision, and will speak unto him in a dream* (Numbers 12:6).

An Extraordinary Answer to Her Question About an Operation

A young secretary approached me, saying that she had been praying for guidance as to whether she should have her foot operated on or not. She had had a recurrent dream for five consecutive nights, in which each time a man appeared and said, "See the man with the *I Ching.* *" She came over to the table where I was writing and said, "I notice you are reading the book *I Ching.* I have never heard of it, but my dream must be significant."

The I Ching, or Book of Changes, Wilhelm/Baynes Edition, Bollingen Series XIX (New Jersey: Princeton University Press, 1950).

I explained briefly the principle of mathematics behind the *I Ching,* and her question was: "Will I get a healing of my foot through osteopathic manipulations and ultrasonic therapy?" The answer was; "Deliverance"—a very positive yes. She was more than delighted, and exclaimed to me, "This is a most wonderful answer, and I feel in my heart it is true. I visited an osteopathic doctor yesterday, and he said I could be healed."

She was seeking an answer, and her subconscious dramatized the answer in a dream recommending the *I Ching.* Why? No one knows. Isaiah says, *As the heavens are higher than the earth, so are my ways higher than your ways* (Isaiah 55:9).

The Psychic Perception Banishes Loneliness

About three years ago on a visit to this island of Hawaii, a waitress spoke to me of her loneliness and inability to meet the right man. I outlined to her a very old but simple technique of impressing her subconscious mind. Following my instructions, she began to imagine the tangible reality of a marriage ring on her finger every night before going to sleep. She did this over and over again, lulling herself to sleep feeling the wonder of it all as an accomplished fact. Feeling the ring on her finger implied to her that she was already married to the ideal man who harmonized with her in every way.

This young lady introduced me to her husband this afternoon by the swimming pool at the Kona Inn. They are ideally married. She pointed out to me that she had conveyed the simple technique outlined above to her two sisters, who also attracted wonderful husbands. Repeating a simple act such as she did over and over again conveys the idea to the subconscious mind* and the wisdom of the subconscious

---

*Dr. Joseph Murphy, *The Power of Your Subconscious Mind* (Englewood Cliffs, N.J.: Prentice-Hall, Inc., 1963).

responds in its own way, bringing the young lady and her future husband together in Divine order. This is psychic perception, or to rephrase it, "The Law of Attraction in Action."

The One-Word Magic Formula

Many people who come to me for advice regarding financial lack and insecurity make the following statement in common: "There is nothing wrong with me that $50,000 will not heal." I give them a very simple formula, which I call my "one-word formula." It is called *wealth*. I ask each one, "Do you believe in wealth?" and invariably each one says, "Oh, yes, of course. I see wealth everywhere," or words tantamount to the same thing.

I elaborate along these lines: "If you look around you as you walk down the street, you see temples, churches, banks, stores equipped with all manner of merchandise, millions of automobiles, trucks and countless machines and equipment of all kinds, all of which came out of the mind of man. Every device and invention such as radio, TV, automobile, typewriter, sewing machine, homes, and skyscrapers were once invisible; but man had an idea or a thought-image in his mind, and nourishing the idea mentally and emotionally, his subconscious mind compelled him into action. Moreover, he attracted everything necessary for the realization of his dreams. There is enough material in the world to clothe every man like a king and every woman like a queen. Moreover, nature is lavish, extravagant, bountiful, and wasteful. Look at the untold treasures in the bowels of the earth, in the sea, and in the air that have not yet been tapped."

After such preliminary discussion on the subject of wealth, my listeners begin to perceive that wealth is of the mind—just an idea or a thought-image—and that when this idea is energized and vitalized, the subconscious activates the conscious mind of the individual, and the law of attraction attracts riches to him—spiritual, mental, and material. The modus operandi is extremely simple: men and women are instructed to lull themselves to sleep every night with just one word, "wealth," knowing what it means and the purpose of it.

As they slowly, quietly, and feelingly repeat "wealth" over and over again prior to sleep, they succeed in conveying the *idea* of wealth to their subconscious minds. The latter respond by revealing oftentimes hidden talents which open up new doors, by presenting them with new ideas, inventions, or discoveries, or by guiding them to treasures of the earth as well as to the spiritual and mental treasures within themselves.

The results have been outstanding and exceedingly successful in all those cases where people faithfully followed the instructions. The few who failed had to be corrected in this technique, because in the waking state they were in the habit of denying wealth; in other words, they were denying that which they were affirming and thus were neutralizing their good. When they corrected this, results followed. When a thought came to them such as "I can't meet that note at the bank," or "I can't afford that new car," they would affirm immediately, "Wealth is mine now" again and again. After a while the idea of wealth became a habit—and it should be observed here that praying is a habit, and that your subconscious is the source of all habit. But wealth is a good habit and poverty is a very bad habit, and that is all there is to the difference between wealth and poverty.

Try the One-Word Formula; It Works

A geologist friend of mine was sent some months ago to Australia to explore the mining situation in the western area. The section had been mapped out for him, but he was not told about two top geologists who had previously explored the area with all the necessary equipment and who had reported back to their headquarters, "No success." My friend discovered a silver vein and uranium deposits the second day he was in the outlined area.

Every night prior to going to Australia, he had lulled himself to sleep with one word, "wealth." His subconscious revealed to him where wealth was, and when he landed by plane in Australia, he was guided right to a mine (which will be developed later on). The same geologist also discovered oil and other treasures of the earth. He knows that wealth is within the mind,* and having found it there, he is directed to its location in the soil or wherever it may be. The other geologists had no inner wealth, and the wealth of the ground eluded them.

How a Secretary Used the One-Word Formula

I was pleased to hear a secretary who comes to my lectures on Sundays at the Wilshire Ebell Theatre in Los Angeles say, "If someone had told me a year ago that I would be driving a Lincoln, wearing a mink coat, expensive diamonds, and sapphires, and be living in my own home and married to a wonderful man, I would have laughed out loud." This young lady took my instruction seriously, saying that it made sense to her and that she decided to use it. She kept her own counsel lest her girl friends in the office ridicule her idea. Three months after her faithful impregnation of her subconscious mind, wealth and happiness flowed to her in avalanches of abundance.

How to Develop Psychic Perception

Every night relax your body as follows, by affirming quietly: "My toes are relaxed, my feet are relaxed, my ankles are relaxed, the calves of my legs are relaxed, my thighs are

---

*Dr. Joseph Murphy, *Your Infinite Power to Be Rich* (West Nyack, N.Y.: Parker Publishing Company, Inc., 1966).

relaxed, my abdominal muscles are relaxed, my heart and lungs are relaxed, my neck is relaxed, my hands and arms are relaxed, my head is relaxed, my eyes are relaxed, my brain is relaxed, my whole being is relaxed, and I am at peace." These affirmations relax your entire body in a wonderful way.

In this relaxed state, you are enabled to implant the following ideas in your subconscious mind prior to sleep: "Infinite Intelligence in my subconscious mind reveals to me everything I need to know at every moment of time and point of space. I am Divinely inspired and Divinely guided in all my ways. Divine guidance is mine now. I always recognize the *lead* which comes to my conscious, reasoning mind. I intuitively perceive the truth about every situation. I hear the truth, I see the truth, I know the truth. I see clearly the motivation of others, and if they are ulterior, I transform them by realizing the presence of God's love, peace, and harmony where the discord is. Divine harmony is mine now. Divine success is mine now. Divine right action is mine now. Divine law and order are mine now. Divine peace fills my soul now. Divine love saturates my entire being now. I am illumined by the wisdom of God, and I am clairvoyant and clairaudient from a spiritual standpoint. The only voice I hear is the inner voice of God, which speaks in peace, and my clairvoyance is my capacity to see peace where discord is, love where hatred is, joy where sadness is, peace where pain is, and life where so-called death is."

What thou seest, man, that too become thou must—
God if thou seest God and dust if thou seest dust.

POINTS TO REMEMBER

1. A boy of about 12 years of age ran home and told his mother, "Mom, papa is dead. I saw him and talked to him." His father's death was later confirmed by long distance phone. It should be realized that every person has these psychic capacities. This

boy had a clairvoyant vision of his father, who appeared to him and said, "Good-bye."

2. You are psychic. How often have you thought of a person and then heard the phone ring, and, behold, you knew it was your friend calling; or you may have sensed that someone close needed you, and when you called on the person, you discovered your intuitive sense was accurate.

3. A woman who was slowly dying due to her belief that someone in Tahiti had put the "fix" on her, healed herself of this fear by filling her mind with this great truth: "I am alive with the Life of God."

4. When you pray for another person, you do not send any healing wave or thought-wave to anybody. It is best to have a deep, inner feeling, an awareness or conviction that the Healing Love of God is now resurrected in the subconscious of the other person, and you will get results.

5. A taxi driver who was praying for prosperity had a vivid dream in which a sage appeared to him, showed him a certain area of land near the Kona Coast in Hawaii, and instructed him to buy it. He did so, and today it has increased 15 times in value. A dream can make you independently wealthy.

6. A secretary praying for guidance had a recurrent dream in which each time a man appeared and said, "See the man with the *I Ching.*" She visited me and asked this question of the *I Ching:* "Will I get a healing of my foot through osteopathic manipulation?" The answer was: "Deliverance," which proved to be true. Her subconscious dramatized the answer in a dream recommending the book, *Secrets of the I Ching.* *

---

*Dr. Joseph Murphy, *Secrets of the I Ching* (West Nyack, N.Y.: Parker Publishing Company, Inc., 1970).

7. Wealth is of the mind—just an idea or a thought-image—and when you repeat the one-word formula, "Wealth," over and over again, you vitalize it and your subconscious mind sets the law of attraction into operation, attracting to you spiritual, mental, and material riches.

8. You must never deny what you affirm, as this would neutralize your good. When a thought comes to you, such as "I can't afford a new car," affirm immediately, "Wealth is mine now," again and again, and after a while the idea of wealth will be impressed in your subconscious mind.

9. A geologist lulled himself to sleep every night with one word, "Wealth." His subconscious revealed to him where wealth was, and he was guided to the right location where he found the treasures of the earth.

10. A secretary affirmed frequently as follows: "I am driving a luxurious car, and wearing a mink coat and expensive diamonds and sapphires, and I am living in my own home and happily married." At the end of three months, all these things came to pass due to her faithful impregnation of her subconscious mind.

11. You can develop psychic perception by affirming quietly: "My toes are relaxed, my feet are relaxed, my ankles are relaxed, the calves of my legs are relaxed, my heart and lungs are relaxed, my neck is relaxed, my hands and arms are relaxed, my brain is relaxed, my whole being is relaxed, and I am at peace." These affirmations relax your body and help develop your psychic power in a wonderful way.

2

The Psychic Powers Within You

Everyone possesses psychic powers, i.e., is aware of events and experiences transcending the five senses. As I was writing this chapter, I received a letter from a sister of mine who belongs to a teaching order of nuns in England. In the letter she stated she saw clearly a group of people in my home silent and praying on Christmas Eve. She looked at the clock (in her dream), and it said 12:00 o'clock, and over the clock was the sign "Beverly Hills."

For the past 21 years I have had a group of friends who celebrate the age-old Mystic Christmas with me, and exactly at midnight we enter into a prolonged silence, meditating on certain age-old truths. My sister was asleep in England but witnessed the whole drama and heard my instructions to the group prior to the silence. There is only one mind, so prior to sleep, as she was thinking of me and the time difference, she simply tuned in at our midnight meeting and saw and heard the religious drama.

These powers are in all people, but oftentimes they are neglected, scorned, and ridiculed. Remember a simple truth: you *automatically* develop your psychic powers as you grow spiritually through prayer, study, meditation, and mystic visioning.

Developing Your Psychic Powers

Be careful to see to it that whatever psychic powers you have are used to bless, help, heal, and inspire mankind. Never use these powers to take advantage of any person or to interfere in any way with a person's right to life, liberty, and the pursuit of happiness. To misuse the powers of your mind would cause a disastrous reaction in yourself for the simple reason that you are the only thinker in your universe, and your thought, being creative, will bring into your own life what you affirm or believe about the other person.

How to Reverse the Negative Pattern

I had interviewed a young woman who was emotionally disturbed over a pending divorce. During the meditative period which followed the close of the consultation, I entered into a very passive, psychic, and receptive state of mind, wherein suddenly a scene opened up before me and I saw this young lady and a companion traveling in an automobile. The car was hit by a truck at a crossroad, the car was demolished, and she and her companion were killed. I reversed the picture in my mind, realizing the Presence of God in her, through her, and all around her, knowing and feeling that she was Divinely guided and watched over by Divine Love at all times.

I asked her, "Are you planning to go home by car for Christmas?" She said, "Something tells me, 'No,' but my girl friend insists I go with her. She will drop me off at my home and will continue to her home a few miles further." I suggested to her that under no circumstances should she go on the journey by car and that she should follow the inner guidance which always seeks to protect her. As a result she cancelled the trip with her girl friend and flew home. Her girl friend went alone and was hit by a truck at a crossroad and fatally injured.

When a psychic picture of a negative nature appears,

reverse it by rising high enough in consciousness. Also, where possible, warn the person, pointing out that guidance comes to all through listening.

Psychical Research

Professor J. B. Rhine of Duke University, the Society for Psychical Research of Great Britain, and many academic laboratories throughout the world have collected a vast body of verified data on thousands of cases dealing with such powers as clairvoyance, whereby one perceives things and situations at a distance; precognition, which is the ability to see future events as happening now in one's mind; telepathy, whereby one communicates mentally with others, collapsing time and space; and retrocognition, which is the ability of many people to see events in the past. All these psychic powers are latent within all of us.

She Read the Obituary Notice Before It Happened

During a recent trip to Kona on the west coast of the big island of Hawaii, I talked with a waitress who told me that from time to time she would inform her family that she had read in the local paper of the deaths of certain very elderly relatives. Each time a complete search of the papers mentioned by her failed to reveal any such notice. Usually a week to ten days later the notices she referred to would appear in the newspapers. This is called precognition.

In her early youth, her Hawaiian mother had told the child that she would be able to see future events just as she had always been able to do, and undoubtedly this made an indelible impression on her subconscious mind, which responded accordingly. Being in telepathic rapport with her relatives, she picked up like a receiving station the impending transition of her relatives, which was known by the subconscious mind of each.

Extrasensory Perception Saved His Father's Life

One day about six months ago, a radio listener of mine wrote me, saying that he was driving his car along the highway to San Francisco when suddenly he heard his father's voice in his ear, saying, "Son, pray for me. I have had a massive heart attack." He pulled over as far as he could to the side of the road, stopped the car, and prayed for his father, affirming, "The peace of God rules in my father's heart. God is healing him now and God watches over him." He said that he silently prayed like this for about half an hour and suddenly felt a great sense of peace.

In the next town, he phoned his father's home, and his mother told him that his father had been taken to the hospital due to a bad heart attack while driving his car to work. Fortunately, he had been able to stop his car, although in the middle of the road, and the man behind him on the road happened to be a medical doctor, who got out of his car, gave him an emergency injection, and took him to a hospital nearby. She said that he had passed the crisis and that he had said to her, "I sent word to my son, and I know his prayers saved my life."

This is clairaudience, whereby you hear clearly the inner voice of intuition or the voice of a loved one perhaps thousands of miles away, as time and space are obliterated in using the higher faculties of your mind. The father had had an intense desire to communicate with his son, who is deeply spiritual, and his subconscious delivered the message in the form of his father's voice to the ear of his son, who was about 600 miles away at the time. The time of the attack and the time the son heard the voice were identical. The quick action of the son undoubtedly saved his father's life.

These powers are within you and can range all over the world without obstruction of time and space.

You Can Send Telepathic Messages to a Lecturer

When I am lecturing on a particular subject on Sunday mornings, there are men and women present who are seeking answers to specific questions or problems. Frequently, they send a message to me on the platform and I find myself deviating from my regular theme in order to answer them, but I always come back to the main topic. After the morning talk, many of them utter words similar to: "I was hoping you would answer the question that was uppermost in my mind and you did." What they do is to project this thought to me on the platform, and I respond. This is called telepathy.

She Said, "I Am Leaving this World"

Recently a woman 92 years of age phoned me and asked me to visit her at a retirement home. On my arrival, she informed me that she was going on to the next dimension in a week's time, and she gave me the time and the day, all of which happened as she predicted. She knew intuitively the moment of her transition, and she informed me that she had been visited by loved ones in the next dimension who advised her they were waiting for her. The next dimension of life interpenetrates this plane, and our loved ones are continuously all around us separated by frequency only. This woman was, as she said, surrounded by a cloud of witnesses and looked upon her transition as going through another door into our Father's home of many mansions. Her parting words to me were, "I go gladly. My three boys will be waiting for me up yonder."

American Society of Mathematics

This distinguished scientific body, after exhaustive checking of the thousands of experiments by Dr. Rhine of Duke University on telepathy, clairvoyance, and precognition, pronounced his findings valid. These extraordinary faculties of the mind today are referred to as parapsychology.

She Heard a Voice Out of the Blue and Found the Will

A widow visited me last year, saying that her husband, shortly prior to his demise, had told her he had made out a new will leaving all of his estate to her. His lawyer knew nothing about a new will; the will he had was ten years old. I suggested to her that she claim, "Infinite Intelligence knows where the will is and reveals it to me." She had searched everywhere in the house, but to no avail. Three or four days after she started praying, however, she distinctly heard her husband's voice in the kitchen where she was doing some ironing: "Look up the 45th Chapter of Isaiah." She did, and there she found the new will, attested to by two witnesses, all in legal phraseology, dated, and signed.

Intuitively she knew that her husband was still alive and much interested in her welfare. She feels his presence quite frequently in the house. Her subconscious mind responded to her prayer and spoke in the voice of her husband, which she instantly obeyed. In the next dimension, conversation is by thought only, but the subconscious mind caused the thought or desire of her husband to come forth as his voice. She experienced the joy of the answered prayer; whether it was her own subconscious mind dramatizing the voice of her husband or the husband's thought made audible by the subconscious doesn't really make any difference, as there is only one mind common to all men and we are all immersed in that one mind.

Talking to the So-Called Dead Is a Common Experience

I visited a local hospital recently to see a man who was, as he said, about to make his transition. The doctors gave him only a few hours to live. We prayed together, and he called out, "Jimmy, Mary, and Jean are here." He conversed with them. These were his three children, all of whom had gone to the next dimension. Then he said to me, "Thaddeus is here. I didn't know he had passed over."

His wife was present and said to me that he was probably raving. He was not raving; he was very rational and conducted a vigorous conversation with me. A week later she learned her son, Thaddeus, had died in Australia. This man actually saw all the members of his family who had passed on. His loved ones were around him, comforting him, undeluded by the concepts of time and space, functioning in fourth-dimensional bodies.

When the scales of superstition and theological brainwashing of thousands of years fall from our eyes, we will see and hear our loved ones, who are all around us, like radio waves carrying television symphonies and voices which permeate our homes inside and outside, but we turn on a dial to prove that the music, people, and voices are really in our room.

An Army Officer Hears His Brother's Voice: "You Will Be Saved"

A few months ago, I spoke at a club dinner, and an army officer sat next to me. He had just returned from Vietnam. He said that he and his brother had been wounded on patrol but that his brother died from the wounds before help could arrive. Then a very strange thing happened. His brother appeared to him and said, "The medics are not far away; I will tell them where you are and you will be saved." In about a half an hour, two medics arrived and administered aid to him. They said, "An officer appeared from nowhere and gave us specific directions." They described the officer and it tallied in every detail with that of his departed brother. After a few hours the helicopter took him to an army hospital, where he recovered rapidly from his wounds.

There is really nothing strange about this when you stop and think things through. You are a mental and spiritual being. When you leave the body, you immediately put on another fourth-dimensional body. You can see and be seen, understand and be understood, and have a perfect memory. In other words, your personality never dies. This brother had an intense desire to save his brother's life. His subconscious mind knew the location of the medics and immediately projected him there, enabling him to be seen by the medics. Also, his subconscious empowered him to speak and issue orders.

Today it is well known in scientific and academic laboratories that you can think, feel, see, hear, and travel, independent of your physical body. In other words, all the faculties of your senses can be duplicated in mind alone. Infinite Intelligence makes no mistakes, and it was, therefore, intended that you use all these faculties transcendentally of your physical body and environment. The subtle body, sometimes referred to as the fourth-dimensional body, can appear and disappear at will, enter closed doors, give messages, move ponderable objects. Remember, you will have bodies to infinity. These bodies are rarefied and attenuated, vibrating at a higher molecular frequency.

There is that in you that was never born; will never die. Water wets it not; fire burns it not; wind blows it not away. It is your Spiritual Self. You go from mansion to mansion, for there is no end to the glory which is man.

POINTS TO REMEMBER

1. Everyone possesses psychic powers and abilities which transcend the knowledge made available by the five senses. There are times when the phone rings and you know who is calling. This is called telepathy. You are picking up the thought of the person who is calling you.

2. In developing your psychic powers, you must be very careful that you use your psychic ability to bless, heal, and inspire others. You must never use your psychic knowledge or power to impose your will on

or take advantage of any other person. You do so at your own peril.

3. When you see a negative pattern for a loved one, a friend, or a client, you can reverse the condition by realizing the Presence of God in the mind and heart of the other. This means to enter into a vivid realization of the presence of Divine love, harmony, and Divine law and order where the person is. Know that the Guidance of God prevails; then you will reverse the negative pattern of the other's subconscious.

4. If while listening to a lecture on mental and spiritual laws, you should desire some specific information regarding your personal problem, project your thought to the speaker, and you will find that he will usually respond.

5. Many people know exactly the time of their transition. They are in rapport with their subconscious mind, which knows all and sees all.

6. The American Society of Mathematics, a most distinguished scientific body of men, have pronounced the conclusions noted by Dr. Rhine's experiments on extrasensory perception as valid.

7. It is possible to hear the voices of loved ones who have passed on to the next dimension. Their desire to give you certain information which you are seeking, such as the location of a lost will, causes their thoughts or desires to be heard clearly. Follow these directions and you will get the desired answer. These are the wonders of your deeper mind.

8. Many people about to pass on to the next dimension will conduct lively and affectionate conversations with loved ones who have long since passed on. The person about to pass on is in both dimensions at the same time and sees and hears his loved ones who are

all around him and who are comforting him. Actually, they are there to bless him and aid him in his transition to the fourth dimension of life, which interpenetrates this plane.

9. It is possible for a loved one who has passed on and who has an intense desire to help you, to appear to those who can aid you and give them the appropriate message.

3

How to Use Extrasensory Perception in Everyday Life

You have frequently heard the term *psychic phenomena*. This was the former designation for what in modern terminology is expressed as *extrasensory perception*. As far back as I can remember, I have heard relatives, friends, acquaintances, and members of my audience tell me about premonitions of events which they felt were going to happen, and happen they did. Countless numbers have told me of dreams and visions which subsequently came to pass exactly as they had seen them happening in their dreams. Many others similarly have told me of seeing apparitions of loved ones who had just passed on at the same moment their forms became visible, and they spoke of the loved ones giving them messages. Many others have heard an inner voice telling them not to take a particular journey or not to marry a certain person.

Many university students who come to see me for consultations regarding emotional or school problems tell me that on numerous occasions they see all the questions in a dream prior to the examination, and they get up immediately and study the answers from their textbooks. All of the foregoing are based on extrasensory perception as they transcend the five senses.

At the Moment of Transition She Appeared to Me

Some years ago while I was talking on the phone to an old friend, my sister walked in through the door. I was surprised and said to her, "Why didn't you tell me you were coming? Did you come by air?" She had been teaching in St. Mary's Convent at Lowestoft, Suffolk, England, and had been a nun for over sixty years. She told me that she had passed on a few moments previously and had come to say goodbye. We conversed for about five minutes. She sat on a chair, was tangible and real, had a body, and wore her habit and rosary beads. Suddenly, however, she melted away and disappeared.

I learned later, taking into consideration the time difference, that she had made her transition that same moment in St. Mary's Convent, Lowestoft, England. We had made a secret agreement that whichever one of us passed to the fourth dimension first would make himself or herself known to the other by appearing and giving a message.

This was not a thought form of my sister, but rather her total personality, as she conducted a vigorous conversation with me, answering questions and describing her physical condition prior to transition, together with the medical diagnosis. Her desire to visit me caused her subconscious mind to project her personality into a new subtle body, which was capable of collapsing time and space, passing through closed doors, moving ponderable objects, and conducting a rational and reasonable conversation. She had a body which was real, solid, and tangible, but it was vibrating at a higher molecular frequency and could disappear and reappear at will.

Extrasensory Travel

I am writing this chapter on New Year's Day. Last night I invited about 30 friends to my home to celebrate the New Year by participating in scientific prayer followed by a prolonged silence. One of the young ladies present said to me after the silent period, "Dr. Murphy, I saw a man behind your back all the time you were giving your audible prayer. He wasn't present in the group when I came in. Who is he? I don't see him now."

She described him in detail, and I explained to her that this was an old friend of mine from Ecuador who used to attend every New Year's mystic celebration with us, but that for the last five years he had been stationed in Spain. I advised her that he had written me, saying that he would be with us on New Year's Eve and would join in our prayers. He had stated that not only would he see us but also that he would be seen. This is not at all unusual. He computed the time, 12:00 P.M. midnight here, when we would go into the silence, and in a meditative state in Madrid, Spain, he instructed his subconscious to project him to my home, where he participated in our prayer therapy.

Just now, as I write this, I have had a long distance call from Madrid, and my friend asked me, "Did you see me last night behind you?" I said, "No, my eyes were closed all the time that we prayed and meditated." But I added that one of our hostesses had seen him clearly and had described him in detail, such as how he was dressed, etc. Her description corresponded in every detail with what he said. He told me the nature of the prayer; said how many were present; stated that he knew only ten of those present, mentioning their names; and said that the others were strangers to him. This is true, because only the ten he mentioned had attended our New Year's conclave when he was stationed in Los Angeles.

He is experimenting in extrasensory travel, and he told me that gradually he is becoming aware of tactile, auditory, and visual capacities in his out-of-the-body experiences. Man is a mental and spiritual being and is omnipresent. When you think of your mother, for example, even though she may be in Hong Kong, you are there with her.

Extrasensory Transmission Solves a Legal Problem

An attorney friend of mine has been trying to solve a prolonged law suit for over five years. He described his difficulties with the people involved and said they were intransigent, recalcitrant, and inflexible, and that finally he had reached what he termed a dead end.

I suggested to him that every night prior to sleep he should imagine that I was there right in front of him congratulating him on the happy ending of the law suit. He was to hear me say to him, "Congratulations for the happy ending. Look at the wonders God has wrought." Every night thereafter he closed his eyes, placed his head on the pillow, and for about ten minutes would fix his attention upon me and hear me vocalize the above congratulatory words. He made it vivid and real and retained in his mind's eye the visualized image of myself and the words which I reiterated over and over again.

At the end of a week, the opposing counsel suddenly agreed to settle amicably and harmoniously. In the meantime, one of the most obstreperous members of the contending party passed on to the next dimension. This attorney, by creative thinking and visioning, succeeded in impregnating his subconscious mind with the idea of a Divine. solution, and his deeper mind brought the solution to pass in its own way.

Remember, the subconscious mind has ways you know not of. Spiritually and mentally I was present, and the attorney used my voice to bring about a conviction in his deeper mind. There is no time or space in the mind-principle; therefore, whenever you mentally dwell anyplace, you are there literally, because you are a mental and spiritual being using your present three-dimensional body as a vehicle; but you have another subtle, fourth-dimensional body that can roam the world independent of time or space.

Extrasensory Communication Joins Two Lovers

A young college girl came to see me one Sunday morning prior to my lecture at the Wilshire Ebell Theatre in Los Angeles, where I speak every Sunday morning. In tears, she said something along the following lines: that she and her boy friend had had a serious quarrel, that he was now somewhere in Vietnam, that she would like to make amends and tell him how wrong she was, and that she would like to hear from him.

I explained to her that she must never impose her will upon another or try to interfere with his life pattern in any way, but that she should first forgive herself and then pray as follows: "Tom is known in Divine Mind, which knows all things. God's love fills the mind and heart of Tom. I surrender him to God, wishing for him all the blessings of life. There are harmony, peace, Divine love and understanding between us. God be with him."

I pointed out to her that when she used this prayer she was blessing the young man and that since Infinite Intelligence is all wise, whatever happened would be good, and that as a result of her prayer they may be drawn closer together or find their highest happiness apart. She understood that she had no right to try to hypnotize or mesmerize her fiance or to mentally coerce him to do her bidding, but that she should turn the matter over to the supreme intelligence in her which knows all and sees all, and that this was the ideal way to handle all such problems.

After the young lady had followed the above prayer process for a few days Tom phoned her from Saigon, mentioning nothing about their quarrel. He told her that she had appeared to him at his tent a few nights previously, smiling, and said to him, "Tom, I love you." Then she had vanished.

The explanation to all this is really very simple. Spirit is omnipresent, timeless, and spaceless. In her prayer therapy, the young girl called upon the love and harmony of God to be resurrected within Tom. When she prayed for him, she was mentally and spiritually present. He, undoubtedly being sensitive and psychic, saw her because she was functioning in a rarefied and attenuated body and was actually there mentally and spiritually and oscillating at a higher degree physically.

Extrasensory Protection Against Voodoo

Recently I received a letter from a waiter in Honolulu, whom I had met on a recent trip there. He said that someone was practicing black magic against him, that he was cursed, and that everything was going wrong in his life. He mentioned the name of the man who he believed was using voodooism or sorcery against him.

I wrote him a lengthy explanation, highlighting and pointing out that all the water in the ocean could not sink a ship unless it got inside; likewise, negative thoughts of others could not enter into his mind unless he opened the door of his mind and gave them entrance; and that God and man are one.

This is indisputable, uncontrovertible, and an eternal truth. God is all there is, and God is absolute truth, boundless love, infinite life, absolute harmony, and infinite joy. I told him that when his thought is God's thought, God's power is with his thoughts of good; that his thought is creative; and that when he thinks of God's love, peace, harmony, and joy, he is automatically protected and immune to all the toxic effluvia of the mass mind. Actually, when he thinks of the eternal verities, it is God thinking through him, and whatever

God thinks can only result in Divine law and order and perfect harmony.

Accordingly, I gave him the following age-old, spiritual prescription, the source of which is lost in antiquity: "Sit down quietly two or three times a day and imagine that you are surrounded by a sacred circle of light. As you continue to do this, after a few days you will actually see a golden circle of healing light all around you. This is an emanation of the God-Presence within you, rendering you impervious to all harm. You are now invulnerable and completely insulated from the fear thoughts or negative suggestions of others. Make a habit of this, and whenever you think of the voodoo man, simply affirm, 'God's Love fills my soul. I loose him and let him go.' "

The sequel to this was most interesting. The waiter continued in the above prayer process, and at the end of a week he read in the paper that this voodoo man had dropped dead on the street, presumably of a heart attack. The explanation to this episode is again very simple. The negative thoughts and imprecations hurled against him by the voodoo practitioner had no place to go, as he no longer received them. On the contrary, he poured out benedictions and orisons on his ill-wisher, and the proverbial boomerang took place. These negative emotions engendered by the voodoo practitioner recoiled with double force back on him, and he actually killed himself.

Remember, you are the only thinker in your universe, and since your thought is creative, what you are thinking about the other you are creating within yourself. When you send out murderous or evil thoughts to another who has insulated himself by God-like thoughts and cannot receive the negative vibrations, they return to you with double force. This is usually referred to as the boomerang. Furthermore, to think or wish evil for another is to kill love, harmony, peace, beauty, and joy within yourself. These thoughts generate emotions, and emotions kill or cure. Evil thoughts plus the emotions generated by them accumulate in your sub-conscious mind, bringing about self-destruction, which can cause a fatal disease; or someone else may be the instrument through which you meet your death, for all murder is really self-murder.

Men, women, and children in this world are simply testifying to our states of consciousness—they are instruments fulfilling our inner attitudes, convictions, and beliefs. According to your belief is it done unto you.

POINTS TO REMEMBER

1. "Psychic phenomena" is an earlier term for extra-sensory perception. Oftentimes you have had an inner feeling and an awareness that the phone call was from a certain person. You have had premonitions, precognitive dreams, intuitive urges which proved to be correct. All of these come under the classification of extrasensory phenomena, which means they transcend the five senses.

2. It is possible for a person who has passed on to the next dimension to appear to a loved one if the individual so desires. The appearance is usually referred to as an apparition.

3. It is perfectly possible for a person who sincerely wishes to travel to meet a friend thousands of miles away to suggest feelingly and knowingly to his subconscious prior to sleep, "I want to visit John Jones. My deeper mind takes over and brings this to pass in Divine order." When you are sincere and come to a definite decision in your mind, your subconscious will project your personality with a fourth-dimensional body to the desired location.

4. There is no time or space in the mind-principle; consequently, you can imagine a loved one or a friend in front of you telling you the good news, that

which you want to hear. Hear it vividly and feelingly, and what you subjectively feel and believe will come to pass.

5. Never try mentally to coerce another to do what you want him to do. If you have a quarrel with a person and you wish him to call you, realize that God guides and directs the other individual and that there are harmony, love, peace, and understanding between you. Whatever happens following this prayer can only be good.

6. You can protect yourself against any negative onslaughts from without by realizing and affirming: "God and man are one, and if God be for me, no one can be against me." God is for you when your thoughts are constructive and harmonious. God's power is with your thoughts of good. You can surround yourself with the whole armor of God and be immunized against all harm. Affirm boldly: "I am always surrounded by the sacred circle of God's eternal love." Busy your mind with this great truth and you will lead a charmed life.

4

How You Can Release
the Psychic Powers Within You

During one Christmas week, I received a wonderful letter from a woman in Northern California, who told me that three months previously her son had vanished from home and no trace of him could be found. The authorities were informed, but he was simply one of thousands of teenagers who have run away to places unknown; results were not forthcoming.

Consequently, she wrote out the mental technique she used, which was as follows: "I went into my boy's room, sat still for about ten minutes and said to myself, 'Infinite Intelligence knows where my boy is, and this supreme intelligence within me knows why he left and reveals the answer to me. It guides me and tells me what to do.' An idea popped into my mind to visit his girl friend, which I did, and she told me they had had a quarrel and she had given him back a ring which he had given her. Then she said he often spoke of going to his cousin's home in Canada. I phoned there at once, and my boy answered the phone. After a short talk he was delighted to come home. There is an intelligence within us all if we would only stir it up."

This woman understood the extent of the powers of her subconscious mind and was aware that when her conscious mind became quiet and relaxed, the wisdom of her subconscious would rise to the surface, revealing to her the answer to her problem. There is an answer to every question and a solution to every problem. Remember, your subconscious knows only the answer. Ask and you shall receive.

Extrasensory Drama Re-enacted and Witnessed by a Doctor

A doctor friend of mine attending a chiropractic convention in Canada was given a beautiful hotel room with an excellent view. Since she was exhausted after a long flight, she dropped off to sleep almost instantly. Suddenly at about 2:00 A.M., she became wide awake with the awful feeling that there was a man in her room, although she knew she had locked the door from the inside. Standing in front of her was a tall man, well-dressed, with a revolver in his hand. He shot himself and fell dead on the floor.

She was petrified with fear and in a state of shock but had presence of mind enough to phone the night clerk, who came rushing up. The doctor hysterically described exactly what had happened. The night clerk then informed her that a man had committed suicide in that room a week previously, and after offering that information, he immediately transferred her to another room.

She asked me how to explain it. I told her that Judge Troward, who had written many textbooks on mental science and who had been a judge in the Punjab of India for many years, once told of a similar incident which his wife had experienced in their new quarters in India. She was awakened by a shot and saw a man who had apparently shot himself dropping before her. She also heard his voice clearly. Though she was emotionally shocked at viewing this grisly event, her husband, Judge Troward, explained it along these lines: that the suicide left an impression, a sort of photographic pattern in the psychic atmosphere, which continuously exists all around us, and a sensitive person could see it reproduced. Mrs. Troward's subjective faculties were activated by the vibrations of the room where it had occurred.

I explained to my doctor friend that it was a thought-form, highly charged with emotion, attached to a particular part of the room where the tragedy had taken place, and that it would be gradually dissipated and fade into nothing. Since this experience, this doctor of chiropractic medicine requests the wisdom of her subconscious mind to guide her to hotel rooms which are harmonious, peaceful, and delightful in all ways, and her subconscious responds faithfully. The emotional atmosphere around the shocking experience at the hotel was completely neutralized, and the explanation of the drama was the cure.

Listen to the Perceptive Flashes of Intuition from Your Subconscious Mind

A banker told me recently that all his important decisions and directions regarding the welfare of the bank and its employees are based on perceptive flashes which come from his subconscious mind to his conscious mind. His technique is praying without ceasing, which means to him that all his thinking is based on principles of life's eternal verities, which never change. He lives in the joyous expectancy of the best, his thinking is constructive, and he has love and good will for all.

"Without ceasing" means an attitude of mind, a deep conviction that God is always guiding and directing him, and this belief on his part causes his subconscious to give him the intuitive flashes of which he speaks. He keeps his mind clear of all negativisms, fear, and discord. Then when he is faced with a problem or a difficult decision, the wisdom of his deeper mind gives him the answer, which transcends his five senses and is always right.

You Are Far More Wonderful than You Ever Imagined

Within your subconscious depths* lie infinite wisdom, infinite power, and an infinite supply of all that is necessary, which is waiting for development and expression. Begin now to recognize these potentialities of your deeper mind, and they will take form in the world without. The infinite intelligence within your subconscious mind can reveal to you everything you need to know at every moment of time and point of space, provided you are open-minded and receptive. You can receive new thoughts and ideas enabling you to bring forth new inventions, make new discoveries, or write books and plays. The infinite intelligence of your subconscious which has the power to heal your body, has a perfect memory of everything you have ever experienced, and can impart to you a vast range of knowledge of an original nature.

Through the intuitive powers of your subconscious, you can attract the ideal mate and the right partner or employee for your business. The wisdom of your subconscious can find the right buyer for your land, your home, or whatever else you may have for sale. It can provide you with ideas worth a fortune, giving you the financial freedom to be, to do, and to travel as your heart desires. Within your subconscious you will find the answer to your most perplexing problems and the cause for every effect. There is an infinite healing presence in your subconscious that can heal the troubled mind and the broken heart. The gold mine and the treasure house of infinity are within you. It can free you from fear

---

*See *The Power of Your Subconscious Mind,* Dr. Joseph Murphy, Prentice-Hall, Inc., Englewood Cliffs, New Jersey, 1963.

and from all kinds of material and physical thralldom and misery.

She Discovered the Healing Presence Within Her

One of many letters I received during the recent Christmas period was from Zurich, Switzerland. The writer was a young lady who had been reading my book *The Power of Your Subconscious Mind,* which is published in German by Ramon R. Keller Publishers, Geneva, Switzerland. In her letter she said that a surgeon had given her about four months to live, but added that with God's help, she could overcome the cancerous condition. Her surgeon suggested that she read the healing miracles of the Bible and continue to practice the techniques given in *The Power of Your Subconscious Mind.* *

She said that for about fifteen minutes three times a day she boldly affirmed with deep feeling and conviction that the infinite intelligence of her subconscious mind, which made all her organs and her entire body, could and would heal her, and she faithfully and regularly pictured in her mind's eye her surgeon saying to her, "A miracle has happened. All clinical tests are negative." Six months passed, and when she went back for a checkup, that is exactly what he said to her. Another six months went by and she received the same assurance. Two years have passed and she says that she is completely cured and back at work. Her surgeon was not surprised at the so-called "miracle" case, for he knows the great truth that all healing is of the Most High.

I have condensed her letter, but the essence of it, which I have given here, shows that any person with a deep, abiding faith and confidence in the infinite healing presence can get results.

---

*Dr. Joseph Murphy, *The Power of Your Subconscious Mind* (Englewood Cliffs, N.J.: Prentice-Hall, Inc., 1963).

Recognizing the Intuitive Feeling
of Your Subconscious Mind

When your motivation is right and based on love and goodwill to all men, and when your mind is free from self-condemnation and self-criticism and you have no desire whatever to take advantage of any person in any way, you will gradually be able to recognize that intuitive feeling which gives you the right answer to your question. The answer may come in many ways, but one of the most frequent is that inner hunch that tells you either to go ahead or to hold back. Your conscious, reasoning mind may try to get in the way, but after you have reasoned the matter out pro and con and then turned the matter over to your deeper mind, full of wisdom and intelligence, you must be alert for the intuitive flash which often wells up spontaneously from your deeper mind. Remember, the impulses, urges, and monitions of your subconscious are always lifeward, as your subconscious mind seeks to heal, protect, and save you from financial loss, accidents, and foolish expenditures of energy and talents. Self-preservation is the first law of life, and this is the law of your subjective mind.

His Inner Voice Saved His Life

Recently a man living in the suburban area of Los Angeles told me that he had been invited by his employer to fly in his private plane for some hunting in the northern part of California. He was on the verge of accepting his offer for the week-end when his inner voice clearly said to him, "Say no," and he obeyed it. Subsequently the plane crashed in a fog and the two occupants were killed.

This man constantly affirms, "God guides me in all my ways." Undoubtedly, he has conveyed this idea of inner guidance to his subconscious, which responds according to the nature of the impression made upon it. This man's premonition was so strong and unmistakable that he said later, "I couldn't fight it."

You Can Develop Your Intuition

You breathe air without effort; likewise, you should learn to let the intelligence within your subconscious mind flow through your intellect without tension. Your subjective mind perceives by intuition. It does not have to reason or inquire, as it is an all-wise and an infinite intelligence. If you say to your subconscious, sometimes referred to as the subjective mind (it is subject to the conscious mind), "Wake me up at 6:00 o'clock," you know that you will awaken exactly at the time specified. It never fails. We must realize that herein lies a source of power which is omnipotent. Many good people have erroneous ideas about the gift of intuition. Many believe that it is an extraordinary event, to be experienced only by highly spiritual people. This is not true. Any businessman or housewife can receive an answer by turning to the infinite intelligence of the subconscious mind, and guidance may be received for any problem.

How to Get a New Idea for Your Sales Program or Your Business

If you are a professional man or an executive of a commercial organization and you want a new idea for your program, try the following technique: Close your eyes, be still, and think of the infinite power and wisdom within you. This will generate a mood of peace, power, and confidence. Then speak in the following simple manner to the creative intelligence within you, which knows only the answer: "Creative Intelligence within me knows all things and it gives me the new idea necessary for this program." Imagine that the creative idea is welling up from your subliminal depths and that it is flowing through your conscious mind. You must not pretend; really believe it. Accept it and then drop it. The latter is the most important and is the secret of the whole process.

After the quiet period, get busy; do something; become preoccupied with routine matters. Above all, do not sit around waiting for the answer. It comes when you think not and the moment when you expect not. The inner voice of intuition speaks like a flash; it is spontaneous and comes unannounced.

Intuition, which means *taught from within,* knows the answer. You must realize that the creative or infinite intelligence which created the cosmos and all things therein contained has no problem; if it had, who would solve them? Therefore, when you seek an answer, be aware that the supreme intelligence in your subjective depths knows only the answer. The amazing suddenness with which the solution sometimes comes is startling. You are transcending your objective reasoning only in the sense of deferring it to a higher guide. After you have received an intuition, you use your reason in carrying it out.

Two Reasons You May Not Acknowledge Your Hunches

The reasons are *tension* and *failure to recognize your hunches.* If you are in a negative, despondent, hostile mood, intuition is impossible. As a matter of fact, only negative direction will prevail. If you are in a happy, confident, joyous mood, you will recognize the flashes of intuition that come to you. Moreover, you will feel under subjective compulsion to carry them out. It is necessary, therefore, to be still and relaxed when you seek guidance, for nothing can be accomplished by tenseness, fear, or apprehension.

Who has not had the experience of being unable to remember a name, then, after dropping the search, have the name come to him later during repose?

The Cultivation of Your Intuitive Faculty
Is of Paramount Importance

For every man and woman, the cultivation of the intuitive faculty is of great significance. Intuition offers instantaneously that which the intellect or reasoning mind could accomplish only after weeks or months of monumental trial and error. When our reasoning faculties fail us in our perplexities, the intuitive faculty sings the silent song of triumph.

The conscious mind is reasoning, analytical, and inquisitive; the subjective faculty of intuition is spontaneous. It comes as a beacon to the conscious intellect. Many times it speaks as a warning against a proposed trip or plan of action. We must listen and learn to heed the voice of wisdom. It does not always speak to you when you wish it to do so, but only when you need it.

If you will only believe, and not just pretend to believe, that Infinite Intelligence is guiding you in all your ways—in your thoughts, words, and deeds—you will be led along the right road. Artists, poets, writers, and inventors listen to their voice of intuition. As a result, they are able to astonish the world by the beauties and glories drawn from this storehouse of knowledge within themselves.

The Meaning of Inner Hearing

The word *intuition* also means *inner hearing.* The oldest definition for *revelation* meant *that which is heard.* Hearing is not the only way to nurture intuition. Sometimes it comes as a thought, but the most common way is to "hear the voice." Many times it is a voice whose texture, color, and substance you can hear as plainly as the voice over the radio. The scientist uses his wonderful gift of controlled, directed, and disciplined imagination, and in the silence he sees fulfillment. His intuition relates to his particular science.

Intuition transcends reason. You employ reason to carry out the dictates of intuition. When you receive intuition, you will often find that it is opposite to what your reasoning would have told you. Begin to practice developing your intuition and let wonders happen in your life.

POINTS TO REMEMBER

1. If you are looking for a person who has disappeared, sit still, quiet your mind, and ask the infinite intelligence within your subconscious to reveal to you his whereabouts. The answer will come to you in ways you know not of. Be alert and follow the lead which comes into your conscious, reasoning mind.

2. A person who has committed suicide in a home or in a hotel room usually leaves a deep, psychic impression in the atmosphere of the particular place, and it is possible for a psychic or similarly highly intuitive person to see the drama repeated as a mental image. The individual has passed on to the next dimension, but has left a descriptive thought-form of his act in the particular location. This psychic photographic impression dissipates itself after some weeks or months, depending on the intensity of the emotional charge behind it.

3. Praying without ceasing means that you think constructively all day long from the standpoint of eternal principles and verities of life. Live in the joyous expectancy of the best, knowing Divine law and order govern your life, and you will be automatically guided to do the right thing. You will recognize intuitive flashes welling up spontaneously, revealing to you the right answer.

4. Your subconscious mind is the storehouse of memory, the seat of your emotions and your intuitive

faculties. Your subconscious mind is one with infinite intelligence and boundless wisdom. The infinite healing presence is within your subconscious, and it knows how to heal and restore you to harmony and peace. It can provide you with the right idea and can free you from limitations of all kinds.

5. The infinite healing presence of your subconscious mind made your body and knows how to heal it. Trust it, believe it, and call upon it, and you will get a response. Don't pretend to believe, but know in your heart that the creative intelligence which made all your organs knows how to heal and restore. According to your faith will it be done unto you.

6. When your motivation is right and you have no desire to take advantage of any person, and when you are praying for Divine law and order in your life, you will receive God's guidance which will cause you to become alert and alive to the intuitive flashes from your subliminal depths.

7. When you make a habit of affirming and at the same time profoundly believing that "God (infinite intelligence) is guiding me in all my ways," often you will hear an inner voice telling you exactly what to do.

8. If you are seeking a new idea for your profession or business, quiet your mind and affirm: "Creative intelligence knows all things and reveals to me the new idea." Then drop it, and the moment you expect it not, the answer will pop into your mind like toast out of a toaster.

9. Fear and tension are two reasons why you do not recognize the answer from your deeper mind. Quiet your mind and contemplate the wonder of the powers within you. When your conscious mind is

quiet and receptive, the answer wells up from the deeper mind.

10. Intuition offers instantaneously that which the intellect or reasoning mind could accomplish only after weeks or months of monumental trial and error.

11. Sometimes the intuitive answer comes as a thought, but the most common way is to "hear the voice," which you can hear as distinctly as the voice over the radio. Begin to practice developing your intuition and let wonders happen in your life.

5

Extrasensory Travel
and Out-of-the-Body Experiences

Some months ago I gave a series of lectures on extra-sensory perception at the Wilshire Ebell Theatre in Los Angeles, and subsequently I received many letters from members of the audience who had had what they termed strange experiences but hesitated to mention them lest they be considered "queer" or "odd" or not all there in mind. I shall mention in this chapter in capsule form the essence, or the gist, of these experiences.

Out-of-the-Body Experience

One woman responded that on Christmas Eve, 1968, she had felt an intense desire to be with her mother in New York City. As she fell asleep, focusing all her thoughts on her former home in New York City, she immediately found herself in her mother's home trying to open the front door. She managed to enter the back door, however, and went upstairs to her mother's room where her mother was lying awake in bed reading the paper. Her mother was startled and asked, "Why didn't you let me know you were coming? I heard you come up the stairs; I knew it was you." This woman kissed her mother and said, "Merry Christmas, Mom. I have to leave now," and she found herself back in her body in Los Angeles. She was able to describe everything in the room, and she had heard the Christmas carols on the radio clearly.

This is not an unusual experience. She was focused on her mother prior to sleep and had developed an intense desire to be with her on Christmas Eve. This desire charged her subconscious mind with a mission, and it projected her personality in a new body 3,000 miles away. Her mother experienced the touch of her lips and hands and heard her voice clearly. She entered through the back door even though it was locked, and sat on a chair by her mother's bed. She was conscious of being out of her body and was aware of a more rarefied body that could pass through locked doors or other material objects.

Extrasensory Travel to Sydney, Australia

An Australian friend told me of an interesting experience he had had on New Year's Eve. On going to sleep, he was thinking of his father's health and began to pray for him by realizing that the Infinite Healing Presence was vitalizing and energizing his whole being, and he began to imagine his father saying to him, "Son, I never felt better in my life. I had a miraculous healing." He kept hearing this over and over again, lulling himself to sleep with the imaginary words of his father, and suddenly he found himself at his father's bedside. He spoke to his father, who was startled by his presence, and exclaimed, "Why didn't you tell me you were coming? What a surprise!"

He said to me that he was consciously aware of and able to see clearly everything in his father's room while realizing that his other body was on a couch in Los Angeles. He appeared to his father fully clothed and had auditory, visual, and tactile capacities outside his body. He was aware that he had a subtle body capable of going through closed doors and collapsing time and space. All this took place in a few minutes, and subsequent letters from his father confirmed his visit in every detail.

Some people would call this an apparition, a ghost, a disembodied entity, etc., but the simple truth is that this man had projected a new body thousands of miles from his home and was able to communicate with and physically touch his father. Man is a mental and spiritual being and will always have a body. A billion years from now you will be alive somewhere functioning at a higher degree of awareness, as life is an endless unfoldment, and your journey is ever onward, upward, and Godward.

Conscious Apparition of a Mother to Her Daughter

Interviewing and corresponding with men and women of all walks of life, I often hear of many extraordinary and fascinating episodes in their lives which they hesitate to discuss with relatives or social acquaintances lest they be considered eccentric, peculiar, or mentally disoriented.

A mother living in Beverly Hills was deeply concerned over her daughter, who was ill in New York City. She informed me that one night she focused all her attention on her daughter, praying for her harmony, health, and peace of mind by realizing the God-Presence was flowing through her daughter as harmony, beauty, love, and peace. The following example illustrates extrasensory projection of her fourth-dimensional body:

She found herself in the private room in the hospital where her daughter was lying awake in bed. Her daughter said, "Oh, mother! I am so glad you came." She and her daughter embraced and kissed each other. The daughter heard her mother's soothing words and felt her embrace clearly. This mother smiled and nodded to the nurse in attendance. Suddenly she decided to return to her body in Beverly Hills, which she saw propped up in bed as she had left it, but she had the distinct awareness of another body to which matter of any kind, such as doors, walls, etc., offered no resistance. Then she re-entered her body.

This type of experience happens to many people who may have great emotional stress and a deep concern to be near a loved one. This is true particularly in time of crisis, when on going to sleep with the dominant idea of being with the loved one, the subconscious mind is impregnated, and they find themselves on extrasensory excursions to the location desired. They are perfectly aware of their physical bodies at the time they leave them and at the time they return to them.

New York Detective Solves Case
Through Extrasensory Travel

While attending the International New Thought Convention in July, 1969, I met an old friend who has been on the detective squad in New York for many years. I gave a lecture on extrasensory perception at that meeting. Subsequently he said to me, "I have something to tell you which will interest you." He had been assigned to a case involving a large robbery, and after three months had not received a single clue. One night in bed he was reading *The Power of Your Subconscious Mind** and fell asleep thinking of the solution to his assignment. Immediately he found himself going through a window in an upstate town in New York State with which he was totally unfamiliar. He noticed three men talking and saw jewels, watches, cameras, and furs

---

*Dr. Joseph Murphy, *The Power of Your Subconscious Mind* (Englewood Cliffs, N.J.: Prentice-Hall, Inc., 1963).

stacked up on tables. He perceived newspapers and their titles, heard the men talking, and decreed to himself, "They will not see me." He looked out the window and saw the street name as well as the name of the theatre which was directly opposite.

Suddenly he realized these were the men he was looking for. There were three rooms in the apartment. He knew he was operating in a projected body which was tangible to him and capable of motion in any direction he wished. He was aware of the magazines that they were reading and knew the town where they were hiding. He said he consciously decreed, "I want to go back to New York now," and immediately he found himself back in his body in his New York apartment.

When he awakened, he called headquarters, and they alerted the local police in that town. They found all the stolen goods and arrested the three men, who were startled to find six fully armed policemen in their apartment at 3:00 A.M. This detective told me that he had told his department he had received a *tip* as to their whereabouts, adding that if he had informed his superiors of his extrasensory travel they would have suggested he go to the Department psychiatrist for observation and treatment.

To be able to account for this solution on the part of the detective, I am convinced that due to his emotional energy being directed towards a solution prior to sleep, he had activated the wisdom of his subconscious mind, which projected his personality in a subtle body in which he was able to see, hear, travel, and understand everything going on around him as well as to direct its own mobility at will. Also, he had the intelligence and reasoning capacity to decree that he could not be seen by the thieves whom he was seeking. All this and much more are latent powers of man's deeper mind.

Through Extrasensory Perception
She Knows Her Son Is Alive

During the course of writing this book, I received a very interesting letter from a woman in Arizona in which she stated that her son had been reported missing in Vietnam. She was distraught, wondering whether he was dead or alive. She stated that she was very tense, worried, and torn between her hopes, fears and growing despair. One night however, she began to read *The Power of Your Subconscious Mind*** and asked her deeper mind prior to sleep, "Tell me whether my son is dead or alive." Immediately, in the sleeping state, she had a clairvoyant vision of her son, who stood out prominently. She saw his bare feet and long beard and the prison walls which surrounded him and the cot on which he slept. She discerned the details of his environment and knew intuitively he was alive and well.

Subsequent information which she received revealed that her son had been taken prisoner, and she later received a letter from him which was surreptitiously smuggled out of the prison. Her subconscious had revealed the answer to her in its own way, and to her it was unmistakable evidence.

Extrasensory Perception Reveals Lost Topaz

A doctor friend asked me if I could help her to recover her lost ring through prayer. This treasured heirloom had been handed down through the family for generations and was of great value. Oftentimes on going to sleep, I concentrate on a request which someone has brought me during the day. In order to do this, I have a clear impression of the person, of our interview and the nature of the problem, and then I affirm something like this: "Infinite Intelligence knows where that topaz is, and it reveals the answer to the

---

*Dr. Joseph Murphy, *The Power of Your Subconscious Mind* (Englewood Cliffs, N.J.: Prentice-Hall, Inc., 1963).

doctor and to myself in Divine order. I accept the answer." I then drop off to the deep of sleep knowing that the answer is mine now.

While I was asleep, in this instance, a scene flashed before my vision similar to a motion picture moving on the screen, and I perceived a woman of foreign origin wearing the ring and asking an older woman, presumably her mother, the value of it. I noticed the color of her apparel, and her hair, which was very gray and hanging down around her shoulders. She had lost some teeth in the front of her mouth and there was a mole on her face.

I phoned my doctor friend in the morning and told her of my experience. She exclaimed, "You described my maid perfectly. She has been with me for 20 years. She couldn't do that. It can't be." I suggested that she tell the maid what her minister said and what he heard her say to her mother, and she did. The maid shed copious tears and said that she had taken the ring merely to show it to her mother and that she had no intention of keeping it; however, the doctor had searched everywhere for it for two months and the maid had helped her in the so-called search, while all the time knowing in her heart that she had stolen it.

My subconscious had revealed the truth about the situation. Its ways and responses are past finding out.

Dr. Phineas Parkhurst Quimby of Maine Experiments with Clairvoyance and Extrasensory Travel in May, 1862

I will relate an experiment that I performed with my subject Lucius in mesmerism. I asked any person in the room to give me the name of an individual written on a slip of paper. I would send the boy to find the person dead or alive, which he would do bringing him into the room and describing him to the audience. On one occasion a name was handed to me which I gave as usual to the boy.

He said this was a man who had a wife and three children, that he left town between two days, was a carpenter by trade, and had left his chest of tools in a barn and had gone direct to Boston. I told him to follow the man, so he went and said he had found him in Ohio in a cooper's shop where he had died. Still I told him to find him.

Finally he said he had found him and I told him to bring him before the people and describe him. Said he, "Can't you see him, he stands here." I answered the boy that he was in a mesmeric state (he could never understand this but admitted it because I said so). To him there was no change, he had all his faculties and his identity was as perfect as when awake. He expressed fear and joy at what he saw as much as though he had been in a waking state. I said, describe him. He commenced giving a general description and I stopped him saying if there was any peculiar trait or feature about him, to mention it. "Well," said he, "I should think anyone might know this man by his harelip." I asked the person who gave me the name if this description was correct and he said it was in every particular. Here was a clear case of spiritualism. The subject would read sealed letters, he would go to a distant place and ask a person a question and get an answer, and yet the person would not be aware of answering any question.

The above report is taken from the writings of Dr. Phineas Parkhurst Quimby written in May,1862. Dr. Quimby knew that there was someone in the audience who was acquainted with the person in question and that his subject Lucius, who was in a mesmeric trance, was clairvoyant and could read the subconscious of the person who knew the missing man, the image of which was in his subconscious mind; and Quimby knew he would reveal his description in detail, including the harelip. Moreover, his trade, family, and where he lived were all known to one or more members of the audience, and Lucius in the trance state simply tapped the subconscious of those present. Quimby used the term "spiritualism" to describe it. Today we would call it "subjective clairvoyance" on the part of his hypnotized subject. One of the abilities of the subconscious is its ease in acquiring information by clairvoyance.

Dr. Phineas Parkhurst Quimby's Experiment in Travelling Clairvoyance

When at Eastport, I put a lady into a mesmeric sleep who wished to go to New Hampshire, to see her friends. I accompanied her. She would smile and bow, and when I asked her to whom she bowed, she said it is our postmaster. She then said we have now got home. She said our folks are looking. I asked her if her father was at home and if she might introduce me and she went through the ceremony. I said ask your father if anything has happened since you left home; at this she started and turned pale and seemed agitated. Upon asking what was the trouble, she said that her uncle was dead, that he was taken sick and had died on such a day and now, mentioning both, also her aunt who came to take care of him had been sick but had recovered and her brother had carried her home. All this was confirmed in a few days by letter. Her uncle Dr. Richardson sent me a letter which I have in my possession, stating that all she had said was literally true.

I might give many experiments of this kind. When I sit by the sick, they tell me their feelings

yet they know it not through their natural senses,
neither am I aware of their presence or feelings
through the natural organs. But every person has
two identities, one has substance and the other the
shadow. To'me the natural man is the shadow, but
to himself, he is the substance and all that he
cannot comprehend is shadow.

A person in a mesmeric state proves to a
person in a waking state that there are two states
and each is a mystery to the other. The one in a
waking state cannot see how a person can be dead
to the waking state and still retain his own identity
and be to himself the same person as before, and
when he comes into the natural state, the mesmeric
state is lost. The mesmerized person cannot understand why the person in the natural state cannot
know what he knows in the mesmeric state. So
each one is a mystery to the other.

Here is the fact. Wisdom has no shadow; a
belief has one. A fact is not a solid: for instance,
there is a stone, that is a fact, and it casts a
shadow. The stone being the invention of man, it is
matter according to our belief, and this belief
makes it a shadow. Man acts either by his belief or
his wisdom. When he is in his wisdom, he is to
opinion a spirit, but to him he is himself with all
his beliefs. So as his belief makes him act in matter,
every act is in his belief and the acknowledging of
matter depends on his belief.

In the above report, written in May, 1862, taken from
Quimby's writings, Dr. Quimby mentions that each one of us
has two identities, which in our modern terminology represent our spiritual nature and our five-sense conditioning
based on our training, indoctrination, environmental influence, and traditional beliefs, but underneath it all is the

Living Spirit Almighty—the Presence of God—and as Dr. Quimby points out, in the mesmeric or hypnotic state, extraordinary powers of our mind are revealed which transcend the intellect and that of our conscious, reasoning mind. He reveals how he sent a young lady who was in a mesmeric sleep on a clairvoyant journey to her home, where she saw everything that was going on at the moment, as well as events such as the death of an uncle which had happened some days previously. Dr. Quimby, who was clairvoyant in the passive state, accompanied her mentally and saw everything she did. Quimby knew that in the subjective mind there is no time or space; therefore, the young woman was in her home in New Hampshire instantaneously.

Such are some of the wonders of the mind which Dr. Quimby brought to light in May, 1862.

POINTS TO REMEMBER

1. Many people have what they term strange, out-of-the-body experiences, which they hesitate to talk about lest they be considered crackpots or be accused of mental aberrations and fantasies.

2. A mother who is greatly concerned about a daughter's illness, who is in a distant city, while concentrating on her daughter prior to sleep, may be projected by her subconscious mind in a subtle body to her daughter's bedside. She can converse with, kiss, and embrace her daughter as well as experience other visual, auditory, and tactile capacities in her fourth-dimensional body.

3. A son living in Los Angeles finds himself at the bedside of his father in Sydney, Australia, and is consciously aware of everything in his father's house. He enters through closed doors and appears to his father, who is startled at his sudden, unannounced visit. Subsequent letters from his father confirm his astral travel in every detail.

4. Frequently, prior to sleep, when you find yourself praying for a loved one or a close friend in whom you are intensely interested, you may find that the person sees you clearly. You also may see the loved one and be able to converse with him as well as describe everything in the hospital room, while at the same time nodding and recognizing the nurse, who, for her part, may also see you clearly and assume you are a relative visiting the patient. You appear fully clothed with all your faculties, as you are a mental and spiritual being capable of thinking, seeing, feeling, and travelling independent of your three-dimensional body.

5. A detective, requesting his subconscious mind to reveal to him the whereabouts of thieves who have robbed several homes, finds himself in their hideout and mentally decrees he will not be seen by them; thereupon, he collects all the data necessary to make an arrest. He finds he is able to move ponderable objects and directs the motion of his subtle body in any direction. He has volition, choice, and initiative. In other words, he is a conscious, reasoning being functioning completely independent of his three-dimensional body.

6. A woman in deep despair, wondering whether her son who was reported missing is alive or dead, decided to ask his whereabouts specifically and believingly of her subconscious mind. Consequently, in the sleep state, she became clairvoyant and saw her son, garbed as a prisoner, in Vietnam, and even the contents of his cell, and was immediately aware that he was alive and well. Subsequent events corroborated her extrasensory experience.

7. A doctor who had lost a very valuable topaz asked the author to help her locate it through prayer. In the dream state, I saw a foreign looking woman

wearing the topaz in question, heard her conversation about its value, saw the mole on her face and observed that three front teeth were missing. When I described the woman to my doctor friend, she realized at once it was her maid who had stolen the ring and she recovered it easily.

8. Dr. Phineas Parkhurst Quimby, in 1862, conducted experiments in travelling clairvoyance. In one instance he hypnotized a woman, who became clairvoyant, and he sent her to her former home, where she reported accurately everything going on, introducing him to the postmaster as well as revealing the death of an uncle and other intimate details, all of which were subsequently verified in detail. Quimby followed her on her mental journey, as he was clairvoyant without going into a trance state. He demonstrated the supernormal powers of the mind.

9. In another instance, Dr. Quimby demonstrated that his subject, Lucius, who became clairvoyant in the trance state, could graphically portray in detail a man who was missing, describing him, his occupation, members of his family, his movements and whereabouts. Dr. Quimby knew that some member of the audience was acquainted with the man in question, and Lucius, in the trance state, simply tapped the subconscious mind of the questioner, who had a complete memory picture of the missing man and knew all about him. These are the wonders of your subconscious mind.

6

Extrasensory Perception and Healing

One of the most interesting and fascinating faculties of the human mind is that of prevision, or the capacity to visualize a future event before it occurs on the screen of space. During consultation work and while conducting interviews with people in many walks of life, I have been informed of remarkable healings and the saving of loved ones' lives through extrasensory perception.

How a Mother's Prayer Saved Her Son's Foot

I interviewed a woman a few weeks ago regarding a domestic problem, and during the consultation she told me about an interesting and remarkable episode in her prayer life. Her son had phoned her from a Vietnam hospital, asking her to pray for him. He told her that his foot was gangrenous and that the surgeon thought he would have to amputate it. But the son had said to the surgeon, "My mother prays for people and they get well." The doctor had encouraged him, saying, "Go ahead. Call her."

She said to me that she sat still after the phone call, mentioned her son's name and affirmed: "My son is known in Divine Mind. God in the midst of him is healing him now, and I give thanks for the action of God which is taking place now." She quietly affirmed this simple prayer over and over again in a quiet, passive, relaxed manner, and after about one hour she fell asleep. In a dream she saw her son and he spoke to her, saying, "Mom, I'll keep my foot. It is wonderful!" She awakened in the morning with a great sense of peace and tranquility. Subsequent news from her son confirmed her deep conviction in the healing power of God.

This mother knew there was no time or space in the mind principle and that her deep realization of the Infinite Healing Presence would be resurrected in the subconscious of her son thousands of miles away. Her favorite Bible verse which she used was: *What things soever ye desire, when ye pray, believe that ye receive them and ye shall have them* (Mark 11:24).

How a Wife's Dream of Her Husband's Heart Attack Helped Avert a Tragedy

While writing this chapter in between interviews, I find I get a lot of rich material from listening to people who have had extraordinary experiences with extrasensory perception, and who hesitate to mention their experiences to their closest friends and relatives lest they be ridiculed or thought of as "a little off the beam."

This brilliant young wife who came to see me about how she should pray scientifically for her young son, told me that a few weeks ago she had fallen asleep after lunch on her divan and had had a very disturbing dream. She felt she was seeing her husband driving his car on the way to Las Vegas, and he was clutching his heart while the car was careening out of control.

Suddenly she awoke with a sense of fear and trepidation and with apprehension of disaster. She opened the Bible and read aloud the 91st Psalm, the great psalm of protection, changing the tense to the present, and prayed for her husband for about a half an hour, starting off with: "He dwells in the secret place . . . He abides under the shadow of the Almighty . . . His angels watch over my husband, to keep him in all thy ways," and other passages, such as, "God is healing him now" and "God's love flows through him, making him whole and perfect." Gradually a sense of peace came over her.

Later in the day she learned that her husband had had a severe heart attack and had lost consciousness. A passing motorist had come upon the car motionless in the middle of the road with a man slouched over the wheel. He investigated and discovered some heart pills in the driver's hand, which, obviously, he was about to take when the sudden attack immobilized him. The motorist put a tablet in the mouth of the stricken motorist and transported him to the hospital, where he had a remarkable recovery in a very short period of time. The motorist told her that it seemed a miracle how the car had come to a stop, as her husband's foot was not on the brake and he was completely unconscious.

This woman's prayer that "angels watch over her husband" acted in the mind of the passing good Samaritan, and he proved to be an angel of mercy and compassion. This wife's prayer and deep, abiding conviction in the Infinite Healing Presence which indwells all of us, acted on the subconscious of her husband 100 miles away, bringing about an appropriate rescue and a remarkable healing to his damaged heart. She added that cardiac tests revealed what the doctors termed a remarkable recovery.

How Clairaudience Saved a Platoon of Soldiers

On a plane trip to New York last year, I sat next to an officer who had recently returned from Vietnam, and during our conversation he informed me about his experience with extrasensory perception and about the voice he had heard from "nowhere." He and his men were under orders to conduct a reconnaissance in a certain jungle area. As they walked slowly along, he heard his sister's voice say clearly and distinctly, "There's a mine in front of you. Stop! Stop! Stop!" Immediately he issued the order to halt, and they found a land mine secreted a few yards away. Undoubtedly, they would have been mangled or perhaps even killed had they gone ahead.

His sister was a nun teaching in a convent in Ireland, and he said that she prayed for him regularly every night and morning as well as at daily mass, always claiming, "The Lord is my brother's light and his salvation."

From the standpoint of geography, this officer knew that his sister was thousands of miles away. Having a degree in psychology, he realized that the voice he had heard was a warning from his own subconscious mind, which sought to protect him and which indubitably had responded forcefully to his sister's prayer. The urges, whisperings, monitions, and intuitions of your subconscious mind are always lifeward. They seek to protect you at all times, as self-preservation is the first law of nature. Be sure to listen to that inner prompting, that silent, inner knowing of your own soul.

In times of great emergency or acute danger, often you will discover that your subconscious mind projects the voice of a person whom you will immediately obey and accept as true. The inner voice which seeks to protect you would, therefore, not be the voice of someone you disliked or distrusted.

Extrasensory Perception and Healing in the Bible

The centurion sent friends to him, saying unto him, Lord, trouble not thyself: for I am not worthy that thou shouldest enter under my roof. . say in a word, and my servant shall be healed (Luke 7:6,7).

Here is a technique of absent treatment, or extrasensory healing. You are told how to pray for another or send your word and heal him. When you pray for another or give what is termed a mental and spiritual treatment, you simply correct what you hear and see in your mind by knowing and feeling the other's freedom, wholeness and peace of mind.

Your *word* in Bible language is your deep, abiding faith and conviction in the response of the infinite healing presence to your belief.

This is how you send the word to heal or help the other person: The first thing you do is think of all that you know about God, such as, "God is boundless love, absolute harmony, infinite life, all powerful, all bliss, the living spirit almighty within me." Realize that there is nothing to change but your thought. Do not use force or mental coercion of any kind. Let go, relax, realize you are a channel resurrecting the wholeness and harmony of the infinite from the invisible to the visible.

When praying for another, affirm quietly: "God is the only Presence and Power. I claim, feel and know that the uplifting, healing and strengthening power of the Infinite Healing Presence is flowing through John or Mary, making him or her whole, relaxed, and perfect. I claim and know that the harmony, beauty, and life of God are now being manifested in you as strength, peace, vitality, beauty, wholeness, and right action." Feel the truth of what you affirm, and as you get a clear realization of this, the sick condition will dissolve in the light of God's love.

The test of your faith and confidence is a mental state of rest and serenity. Maintain the quiet mind and pray again for the person when you feel guided to do so; gradually, you will build up a conditioned state of mind, and the day breaks and all the shadows flee.

The Dying Man Sat Up and Began to Speak

Recently I gave a lecture at the beautiful Religious Science Church in Oakland, California; and while there, a man visited me in the hotel for the express purpose of finding out how he and his wife should pray together. During the course of the interview, he spoke along these lines: that he believed in the powers of the subconscious mind,* and that he had read the book over and over about 15 times, and furthermore that he had diligently practiced what he had read.

His son, who is of the Evangelical Church, and who takes the Bible literally, was very ill, actually in a comatose condition for a few days. Not too much hope was given by his doctors, though they did everything possible for him and were very kind and considerate.

One day as this man prayed for guidance, he visited his son, who didn't seem to recognize him and lapsed off into a lethargic sleep. The father said out loud to the son's subconscious, "Son, Jesus is right here now and you see him. Jesus is going to heal you now. He is putting his hands on you now. You feel the touch right now."

He repeated these statements several times slowly, gently, and positively. His son was unconscious when he spoke and apparently was not aware of his father's presence. After about ten minutes, the son sat up in bed, opened his eyes and said, "Hello, Dad. Jesus came and touched me. I know I am healed. He said to me, 'I say unto thee, Arise.' " His son was discharged two days later, completely healed.

What happened? This boy's subconscious mind accepted his father's statement that Jesus was there and his subconscious mind projected the thought form; i.e., this boy's religious concept of Jesus was portrayed to him while he slept, based on the images in his prayer book, paintings,

---

*Dr. Joseph Murphy, *The Power of Your Subconscious Mind* (Englewood Cliffs, N.J.: Prentice-Hall, Inc., 1963).

church statues, etc. This boy blindly believed that Jesus was there in the flesh and that he had placed his hands upon him. His blind belief was registered in his subconscious, and it responded accordingly.

You can tell a man in a trance that his grandmother is here now and that he will see her clearly. He will see what he believes to be his grandmother. His subconscious projects the image of his grandmother, based on his subconscious memory picture. You can give the same man a post-hypnotic suggestion, saying to him, "When you come out of the trance, you will greet your grandmother and talk with her." He does exactly that.

This is called a subjective hallucination. The faith kindled in the subconscious of this man's son was the healing factor. It is always done unto us according to our faith or mental conviction.

The Resurrection of the So-Called Dead

The subconscious is amenable to suggestion even though the subject is unconscious. The deeper mind can receive and act upon the suggestion of the operator. In a sense, you could call such an incidence the *resurrection of the dead*. It is the resurrection of health, faith, confidence, and vitality.

The Woman Refused to Consult a Doctor of Medicine

A woman phoned me from New Orleans, saying that she felt very weak and had collapsed three times during the week after some slight exertion in her home. I suggested that she consult a doctor at once and get a checkup, and that she pray both for him and for herself, while being continuously aware that God is guiding her and her doctor, and that God in the midst of her is healing her now.

She said, " I hate doctors, nurses, and pills. My husband insists I go to a doctor, but I believe God can heal me." I explained to her that while being full of hate, she is thereby blocking the healing stream of love and joy, and that she must let the sunshine of God's love enter into her heart. Her mental resistance sets up a resistance to the Healing Presence and a short circuit takes place. She was adamant, saying, "I'm not going to any doctor." Her husband later told me that that same day she collapsed suddenly and was rushed to the hospital, where she died of coronary thrombosis.

Her husband had been begging her to submit to a medical examination. If she had done so, her condition would have been discovered, and, undoubtedly, alleviated. Her life would have been prolonged. Right medical care plus prayer therapy, working together, would have blessed her in many ways. God indwells the doctor, the dentist, the osteopath, and the chiropractor. Every man is a temple of the living God.

Why You Should Honor the Physician

In the Book of Ecclesiasticus, Chapter 38, Paragraphs 1 and 2, you read these words:

> *Honour a physician with the honour due unto him for the uses which ye may have of him: for the Lord hath created him. For of the Most High cometh healing, and he shall receive honour of the king . . . the Lord hath created medicines out of the earth; and he that is wise will not abhor them . . . And he hath given men skill, that he might be honoured in his marvelous works.*
>
> *My son, in thy sickness be not negligent; but pray unto the Lord, and he will make thee whole . . . Then give place to the physician, for the Lord hath created him: let him not go from thee, for thou hast need of him. There is a time when in their hands there is good success. For they shall also pray unto the Lord, that he would prosper*

> *that which they give for ease and remedy to*
> *prolong life . . .*

These verses are very wise and are saying to you that you demonstrate at your level of belief. If you do not get well by prayer, see a doctor. If you have the conviction of the presence of God where the trouble is, it will disappear; if not, do the next best thing—immediately. If your prayers are successful, health should spring forth speedily. Remember, if you can't grow a tooth or mend a broken bone at once through prayer, better see a dentist for your tooth and a surgeon for your bone. This is common sense and certainly much better than being a cripple for life.

Why the Atheist Had a Remarkable Healing at a Shrine

Healings occur sometimes unheralded at various religious services. Many people have told me that they have had healings at our healing services on Sunday mornings. They add that they did not expect a healing, that they were skeptical, that they were in no state of exaltation, and that they were not even thinking of a healing. From what they say, one would gather that they lacked faith; therefore, the question arises: How could they receive a healing?

The answer is rather simple. All of them, whether atheists or agnostics or believers, are looking for a healing, and their minds are receptive to receive the prayers of the multitude present. Perhaps they are going to a medical doctor, osteopath, or chiropractor for treatment, which is highly indicative that they desire to be healed. Desire is prayer, and God will answer the prayer of an atheist if he believes just as well as that of any religious person, as God with His law is no respecter of persons. Desiring a healing causes a receptive attitude of mind which also causes the idea of perfect health to be resurrected in the subconscious mind. That is what the people present at church or at a shrine are praying for.

When the so-called atheist mentioned in this subtitle mingled with a group of people gathered together in prayer at a shrine, who were affirming that all those present are healed, made whole and perfect, he established a definite psychological and spiritual link with all those present. It is thus possible for him to be healed, as the healing vibrations emanating from all those dedicated people present impinge on the subconscious mind of the atheist, transforming the negative patterns and making way for the healing power of his subconscious to be resurrected. Collective prayer neutralized the mental poisons of his subconscious mind and made way for the spirit of wholeness and beauty to enter in.

POINTS TO REMEMBER

1. Prevision is the capacity of your deeper mind to see a future event before it happens.
2 A mother can pray for a son thousands of miles away; and by dwelling on the thought, "God in the midst of him is healing him now" until her mind is at peace, her conviction of God's healing presence is resurrected in the subconscious of her son; his foot is healed. There is no time or space in the mind-principle, and his mother's inner realization is made manifest immediately in the experience of her son.
3. Husbands and wives are subconsciously linked together. It is possible for a wife to perceive an acute illness of her husband in a dream state and, through prayer, prevent a tragedy. In this case, a wife in a dream state saw her husband have a cardiac attack while driving a car. She turned to prayer, and her prayer was answered.
4. An officer on patrol in Vietnam with his platoon heard his sister's voice saying, "There is a mine in front of you. Stop!" He obeyed instantly and saved the lives of himself and his platoon.

5. When the Bible says, "He sent his word and healed them," it means you don't have to visit the sick person, who may be thousands of miles away. But knowing that mind is timeless, spaceless, one, and indivisible, one can enter into a deep conviction of God's healing power. Your inner knowing and belief will be felt by the sick person, and a healing will follow.

6. A father realized that the subconscious mind of his son, who was in a comatose condition, was amenable to suggestion. He made powerful suggestions to his son, who was unconscious, by affirming, "Jesus is here. He is touching you now. Jesus is healing you now." The boy saw the thought form of Jesus in his unconscious state. Believing it was Jesus, he was healed. His blind belief healed him, as his subconscious will respond whether the object of his belief is true or false. The healing power of the subconscious is the only healing power regardless of all techniques, processes, rituals, ceremonies, talismans, shrines, or frills.

7. When you are sick and when you pray, if you do not get results immediately, go and see a doctor at once.

8. Many religious fanatics refuse to go to doctors when they are seriously ill. In their superstitious beliefs they think it wrong to do so. All this is a mild form of insanity. Extremes are always dangerous. After prayer, health should spring forth speedily; if it doesn't, it means you don't have the faith you think you have. Go to a doctor, bless him, and keep on praying for health and harmony. Remember, your longing for faith is not real faith. Real faith is made manifest right here and now. Countless thousands would be alive today if they had

consulted a doctor in time instead of resenting medical help and in that way blocking a healing.

9. The Book of Ecclesiasticus, Chapter 38, states definitely and categorically, *Give place to the physician for the Lord hath created him . . . for thou hast need of him.*

10. An atheist can get answers to his prayers, for the laws of mind are impersonal. If he is desirous of a healing and is going to a doctor for treatment and visits a healing shrine where people are praying, it is possible for the collective healing consciousness of those praying to penetrate his subconscious, resulting in a healing.

7

Why You Will Live Forever

Thousands of years ago, Job asked, "If a man die, shall he live again?" God is Life, and Life cannot die. Life cannot die. Life has no beginning and no end. Every person walking the earth is God or Life in manifestation.

Your body is an instrument or vehicle through which the life-principle is expressed. You will always have a body of some sort, no matter in what dimension of life you function.

So-called death is not the end; it is only a beginning. You will arrive at your new destination, actually, when you pass on from this three-dimensional to a fourth-dimensional existence, and you will look upon it as a new birth. You will possess a new, fourth-dimensional body which is rarefied and attenuated by our standards, enabling you to go through closed doors, to collapse time and space, and to be where you want to be through the medium of your thought.

Milton said, "Death is the golden key that opens the palace of eternity." The journey of every man is from glory to glory, from octave to octave, and through the many mansions of our Father's house.

When you pass to the next dimension of life, you will see and be seen. You will recognize loved ones. You will possess all your faculties as an individual. When you came into this world, you were met by loving hands, who took care of you; you were fondled, coddled, and cosseted. And what is true on this plane is true on all planes. You will meet loved ones who will care for you and who will initiate you into the activities of the next dimension of life.

Life Is Progression

Your life is an endless unfoldment—ever onward, upward, and Godward. You can't go backward, for the urge of life is progression, expansion and growth. God is Infinite Life. This Life is your life now; therefore, there is no end to your newness, freedom, and spiritual awareness. Never in all eternity could you exhaust the wonders and glories that are within you.

In the 15th Chapter of the First Book of Corinthians, Paul says: *There are also celestial bodies, and bodies terrestrial: but the glory of the celestial is one, and the glory of the terrestrial is another. And as we have borne the image of the earthly, we shall also have the image of the heavenly.*

You Live Forever

In the above-mentioned Biblical quotation, Paul is saying that there really is no death and that all men and women are immortal. Every child born in your home is simply Life taking on that form. This in scriptural language is God (life-principle) coming down from Heaven (invisible state) and appearing on earth, or being made manifest. When your present body ceases to function perfectly, you will put on a fourth-dimensional body, referred to frequently as an astral body, subtle body, celestial body, subjective body, etc. You can't take any earthly possessions with you, but you do take all that you have ever learned and believed about God, life, and the universe; in other words, you take the sum total of your beliefs, convictions, impressions, and awareness.

Fourth-Dimensional Teachers Attend Lectures

Frequently some psychics, clairvoyants, and similarly gifted people speak to me following lectures on Sunday mornings at the Wilshire Ebell Theatre in Los Angeles. They describe men sitting on the platform while I am speaking. I have asked them to describe the men they purportedly saw, and in each instance they have accurately described the following teachers in the next dimension: Dr. Emmet Fox, author of *Sermon on the Mount;* Judge Thomas Troward, author of six books on Mental Science; and Dr. Harry Gaze, author of *Emmett Fox, the Man and His Work.* They have also accurately described my father, who passed on many years ago, as well as my sister and other relatives and teachers. In no instance had these sensitives ever met any of my relatives or the teachers referred to in this chapter; neither had they read any of their works or seen photographs of them.

I do not look upon their perception and experience as unusual, as there is no reason whatever why men and women who are spiritually developed can't attend spiritual gatherings whenever they wish and appear and reappear at will. I have not seen the men and women mentioned on the platform, but several people present who are highly sensitive and clairvoyant see these fourth-dimensional beings frequently on the platform Sunday mornings and sometimes at my classes on the I Ching, Tarot Symbolism, and the esoteric meaning of the Bible.

Spiritually Advanced Individuals
Can Appear and Reappear at Will

Judge Thomas Troward, author of *The Edinburgh Lectures on Mental Science* and many other books, including his foremost book called *The Creative Process in the Individual,* spent the greater part of his life as a judge in the Punjab of India. I quote from *The Creative Process in the Individual* (first published in 1915 by Dodd, Mead and Company), as follows:

Manifestation is the growth proceeding from the principle, that is to say, some Form in which the principle becomes active. At the same time we must recollect that, though a form is necessary for manifestation, the form is not essential, for the same principle may manifest through various forms, just as electricity may work either through a lamp or a tram-car without in any way changing its inherent nature. In this way we are brought to the conclusion that the Life-principle must always provide itself with a body in which to function, though it does not follow that this body must always be of the same chemical constitution as the one we now possess. We might well imagine some distant planet where the chemical combinations with which we are familiar on earth did not obtain; but if the essential life-principle of any individual were transported thither, then by the Law of the Creative Process it would proceed to clothe itself with a material body drawn from the atmosphere and substance of that planet; and the personality thus produced would be quite at home there, for all his surroundings would be perfectly natural to him, however different the laws of Nature might be there from what we know here.

In such a conception as this we find the importance of the two leading principles to which I have drawn attention—first, the power of the Spirit to create *ex nihilo,* and secondly, the individual's recognition of the basic principle of Unity giving permanence and solidity to the frame of Nature. By the former the self-recognizing life-principle could produce any sort of body it chose; and by the latter it would be led to project one in harmony with the natural order of the particular planet, thus making all the facts of that order solid realities to the individual, and himself a solid and natural being to the other inhabitants of that world. But this would not do away with the individual's knowledge of how he got there; and so, supposing him to have realized his identity with the Universal Life-Principle sufficiently to consciously control the projection of his own body, he could at will disintegrate the body which accorded with the conditions of one planet and constitute one which accorded just as harmoniously with those of another, and could thus function on any number of planets as a perfectly natural being on each of them. He would in all respects resemble the other inhabitants with one all-important exception, that since he had attained to unity with his Creative Principle he would not be tied by the laws of matter as they were.

From the above paragraphs, you will glean that an individual who is highly advanced spiritually and who senses his oneness with the universal Life-Principle can project himself to any country or even other planets at will; and the Life-Principle, which is all-wise and all-knowing and which is the only cause and substance, will project a body in harmony with the density of atmospheric pressure of the particular planet; in other words, he would be able to appear and reappear at will.

For example: If you melt ice, you have water. If you continue heating the water, you will have steam, which can be invisible. But steam, water and ice are all one, vibrating at a different molecular wave length. The functions and physical properties of each are different. Likewise, you are spirit, mind and body. They are all one, but each has a separate function. There is nothing illogical about a spiritually developed man living, let us say, in New York City and contemplating himself as being in Johannesburg finding himself in the latter city instantaneously. He is a mental and spiritual being and knows that mind and spirit are omnipresent and that when he focusses on a certain location and decrees he is there, automatically he dematerializes his body, which is composed of atoms and molecules, which now appear invisible like the steam we mentioned. He then condenses down the high molecular vibration to the three-dimensional body and appears walking the streets of Johannesburg. This type of man would also be able to go to the next dimension at will as well as to other planets and to return when he wished to do so.

A Dying Man Talks to His Father, Mother and Son in the Next Dimension

Recently I visited a man who was dying of cancer, which had metastasized over his body. He talked to me about several things and we prayed together. He was perfectly rational in his mind and began to talk to his father and mother, who had left this world many years ago. He said, "They are here and I am going with them." Then he said, "I see John. I didn't know John was there!" Neither did his wife, who was present, know about John's presence. But one week later she received a letter from India, where John (their son) was stationed. John had passed on about the same time that his father made the remark to me at the bedside.

Your Departed Loved Ones Are Right Where You Are

Your so-called dead relatives are all about you, and you must cease believing that they are "dead and gone." They are alive with the life of God and separated from us by frequency only. You do not see cosmic rays, gamma rays, beta rays, alpha rays, ultraviolet rays, or infrared rays. Your physical eyes are blind to the great invisible reality that lies around you. You would see a different world if you began to see through your inner eye of clairvoyance; and in similar manner, what a vastly different world you would see if you were as sensitive as the x-ray machine or infrared rays.

You might say to the writer that there is no one in your room as you read this chapter, but turn the dial of your radio or television set and, lo and behold, you see, or hear, people talking, laughing, and dancing. You hear music, singing, and the voices of men and women perhaps thousands of miles away. All these programs fill the room where you are seated. Man is a broadcasting and receiving station himself; that is why he was able to invent a radio and a television apparatus, because all these powers and faculties are within him, submerged in most people, but still quite active in others who walk the streets of your own city.

Eradicate That Hypnotic Spell

The average man is under a sort of hypnotic spell of belief in death; but when he opens his spiritual eyes and lets the accumulated scales of centuries of false beliefs fall away, he will realize that he has an existence beyond time and space as we know it, and he will see and feel the presence of those whom he now calls "dead."

I have been at the bedside of many men and women during their transition. They have shown no signs of fear. Instinctively and intuitively, they feel they are entering into a larger dimension of life. Thomas Edison was heard to say to his physician before he died, "It is very beautiful over there." All of us have a natural wistfulness regarding the state of our loved ones after they leave this plane of life. We must realize that with the dawn their happy faces smile which we have "loved long since and lost a while."

What the Poets Have Said About the Next Dimension of Life

Tennyson said:

> Thou wilt not leave us in the dust;
> Thou madest man, he knows not why, He thinks
> he was not made to die; and thou hast made him;
> thou art just.

Wordsworth said:

> Our birth is but a sleep and a forgetting;
> The Soul that rises with us, our life's star
> Hath had elsewhere its setting
> And cometh from afar;
> Not in entire forgetfulness,
> And not in utter nakedness,
> But trailing clouds of glory do we come
> From God, who is our home.

Whittier said:

> And so beside the Silent Sea
> I wait the muffled oar;
> No harm from Him can come to me
> On ocean or on shore.
>
> I know not where His islands lift
> Their fronded palms in air;
> I only know I cannot drift
> Beyond His love and care.

Robert Browning said:

> All that is, at all,
> Lasts ever, past recall;
> Earth changes, but thy soul
> And God stand sure;
> What entered into thee,
> That was, is, and shall be;

Time's what runs back or stops;
Potter and clay endure.

All these men are saying the same thing; that is, that life cannot produce death, as that would be a contradiction of its own nature. Life is, was, and shall be.

The Departed Father Returns and Corrects a Wrong

An attorney friend of mine in Mexico told me that his sister had hypnotized their father prior to his transition and had given him a post-hypnotic suggestion that the largest share of his fortune would be given to her. The father, thereupon, acting under the hypnotic suggestion, followed the order given his subconscious mind of which his conscious mind was unaware.

One evening, shortly after the demise of their father, the two were seated in the living room listening to a radio program when their father appeared to them fully clothed and wearing the same house jacket which had become inextricably a part of his dress around the house. He was angry and told his daughter how she had hypnotized him and cheated her brother and directed her to make it right at once, to which demand she immediately assented. In the next dimension of life, the father knew that he had been taken advantage of, and he decided to visit the daughter and correct it. Undoubtedly, his intense desire to right the wrong and bring about his true decision regarding the will charged his subconscious with sufficient intensity to precipitate his personality into their living room.

This was not a ghost or a strange hallucination or thought form, but the entire personality of their father, who possessed all his faculties and who was able to talk and instruct his daughter in righteousness and integrity.

A wonderful, informative, and scientific book to read along similar lines as the above is *Phantasms of the Living* by

Edmund Gurney and Frederic Myers of Cambridge, published
by the Society for Psychical Research, London.

How to Give the Oil of Joy for Mourning

You must never grieve nor mourn for departed loved
ones. Radiate the qualities of love, peace, and joy to the
friend or relative who has passed over to a larger dimension
of life. Lift the other up in your mind and heart and rejoice
in his new birthday, knowing that Divine love and Divine life
are where he is. Realize that the dear ones who have passed
on are dwelling in a state of beauty, peace, and harmony.
You make the loved ones happy by this attitude of mind.
Instead of feeling that they are dead and gone and that they
are where their graves are, feel that the wisdom, intelligence,
and love of God are flowing through them in transcendent
loveliness. Whenever you think of a departed relative or
friend, silently bless him by affirming, "God loves you and
cares for you." This attitude of mind heals all grief and
sorrow for you and yours.

Entering Into a Higher Vibration

There is no one buried anyplace, whether in the soil or
far away at sea. The body is interred and undergoes dissolu-
tion, returning to its primordial elements. Modern, up-to-
date, scientific thinkers never visit graves, as there is nobody
there. To identify with the body in a grave and to put flowers
on the grave is to identify with limitation and finality, which
brings on disease and all kinds of loss to the person who
indulges in this custom. In the modern funeral, there is no
body in evidence, and the relatives meet for prayer and
meditation, celebrating the loved one's new birthday in God
as he moves onward, upward, and Godward.

POINTS TO REMEMBER

1. God is life, and that is your life now. The Life-

Principle hath no beginning and no end; therefore, there is no end to your growth, expansion, and unfoldment. A billion or a trillion years from now, you will be alive somewhere expressing more and more of the wonders and glories within you.

2. You will meet loved ones and other advanced souls in the next dimension who will initiate you there and help you on your journey that knows no end.

3. Life is a constant progression. Life neither goes backward, nor tarries with yesterday. Your journey is forward. It is newness and endless growth from glory to glory.

4. Occasionally, as I lecture on Sunday mornings to a very large audience, several sensitives who are clairvoyant see fourth-dimensional men and women on the platform where I lecture. Their descriptions of them fit exactly these persons as I have known them. These sensitives had never met any of these people in the flesh; people who have advanced knowledge of spiritual and mental laws can go where they want to go, as they are not bound by time or space.

5. Judge Thomas Troward, who wrote many outstanding books on mental laws, points out that as a man advances in his realization of his oneness with the All-Originating Spirit, he can visit other planets as well as any point on earth. He can do this by focusing his attention on the spot he wishes to visit, by disintegrating his present body and causing the All-Originating Intelligence within him to reassemble and coalesce its atoms wherever on this earth or on other planets he projects himself. The All-Originating Intelligence would create a body consonant with the density and atmospheric pressure of whatever planet is selected.

6. Occasionally, men and women who are about to depart from this plane see, hear, and talk to departed relatives who are at their bedside to comfort and aid them in their transition.

7. Your loved ones who have passed over are right where you are; if you were clairvoyant, you could see them and talk to them. They are separated from you by frequency only. If you see a fan oscillating at a very high speed, the blades and the fan itself become invisible. Slow it down, however, and you see the fan. It is the same idea regarding three-dimensional and four-dimensional living.

8. Many of the poets intuitively perceived that man is immortal and that trailing clouds of glory, we come from God, which is our home. In God we live, move, and have our being. God lives, moves, and has His being in us. We are living in eternity now, because God (the Life-Principle) is the reality of each one of us.

9. It is possible for a departed father to reappear to you from the next dimension and give you a message of importance. His intense desire to correct some wrong charges his subconscious sufficiently, enabling him to do this.

10. Never mourn the so-called dead. Protracted grief is selfishness, as you would be thinking of *my* loss, *my* sorrow, *my* grief. Surround the loved one with peace and harmony and realize that God's love flows through him and the joy of the Lord is his strength. This attitude banishes all grief and desolation. Suppose you had gone on first. Realize you are sparing your loved ones all sense of loss, grief, and loneliness. Rejoice in your loved one's new birthday in God. You can't keep loved ones forever. They are loaned to you from God and all must pass on. This is a cosmic law and must be good or it

would not be. Your children are not yours; they come from God through you, but not by you. The child who lived for one hour here or who was born dead still lives and is a grace-note in the grand symphony of all creation.

11. There is no one buried in a grave or vault. Never visit a graveyard thinking there is someone there. This induces lack, loss, and limitation, because you are identifying with finality. The body is not the person. Give the flowers of your heart to the loved one right where you are. Realize the truth of the 23rd Psalm: *Goodness and mercy follow them all the days of their lives because they dwell in the house of God forever.*

8

How Extrasensory Perception Reveals Answers in Dreams

The Bible says: *I, the Lord* (subconscious mind) *will make myself known unto him in a vision and will speak unto him in a dream* (Numbers 12:6).

There are numerous references in the Bible to dreams, visions, revelations, and warnings given to men during sleep. Your subconscious mind is active 24 hours a day and never sleeps. The Bible points out that Joseph was amazingly accurate in his analyses of the dreams of Pharoah, and that his mental acumen and sagacity in predicting the future through the interpretation of dreams brought him praise, honor, and recognition by the king.

Dreams have captivated scientists, scholars, mystics, and philosophers down through the ages. Many answers to man's most acute problems have been given in dreams. Since Biblical days, various interpreters and expositors in every country have been engaged in the analyses and interpretations of dreams. Freud, Jung, Adler, and many other distinguished psychologists and psychiatrists have studied the symbols portrayed in dreams, and by interpreting the meaning to the conscious mind of the patient have released hidden phobias, fixations and other mental complexes.

Your dreams are projections of the contents of your subconscious mind, and in many instances, they answer your problems and warn you regarding investments, journeys, and marriage, as well as pitfalls of daily living. Your dream is a dramatization of your subconscious mind and is not fatalistic. You mold, fashion, and shape your own future by your thought and feeling. Anything in your subconscious is subject to change, and when you know the laws of mind, you predict your own future. Remember your future is your present thinking made manifest, because your subconscious mind faithfully reproduces your habitual thinking 24 hours a day.

The Meaning of the Symbols in Your Dreams

The symbols which appear in your dreams are personal and apply to each individual only; the same symbol appearing in the dream of a friend or other member of your family may have a completely different meaning.

The Dream Reveals a Small Fortune in Dollar Bills

I once had a telephone call from a woman in New York City, stating that her husband had told her prior to his demise that he planned to take a large sum of money from his private safe and invest it in a foreign country for greater returns. A few days later he passed on, and when the safe deposit box in the bank was opened, there was no cash, but there was a record at the bank that two days previously he had visited the vault. There was no trace or record of any investment, and a minute inspection of his desk revealed no clues.

I suggested to her that she turn her request over to her subconscious mind, which knew the answer, and that it would reveal the answer to her in its own way. She prayed as follows prior to sleep: "My subconscious knows where my husband secreted that money, and I accept the answer and believe implicitly the solution will come clearly into my conscious mind." She quietly dwelled on the meaning of these words, knowing they would be impressed on her subconscious, thereby activating its response.

She had a very vivid dream in which she saw a small, black box hidden behind a picture of Lincoln on the wall in her husband's work den. She was shown in the dream how to press a secret button, which could not be seen with the naked eye. When she awakened, she rushed to the den, took down the picture of Lincoln, and when she pressed the button revealed in the dream, an opening appeared containing the black box which in turn contained $50,000 in currency.

She discovered the treasures of her subconscious, which knows all, sees all, and has the know-how of accomplishment. You too can take a similar step in putting your ESP to work in locating a treasure of any type that really belongs to you.

How a Dream Prevented a Great Psychological Shock

A young woman in San Francisco experienced a recurrent dream for four consecutive nights. In her dream, her fiance, who was living in Los Angeles, appeared to her and quite suddenly a very high mountain, which seemed impossible to scale, came between them. In the dream she was deeply surprised, frustrated, and bewildered. She awoke wrestling with the problem and sensing something very wrong and shady.

I asked her what the mountain signified to her, as every dream, when interpreted properly, must coincide with the inner awareness and feeling of the dreamer. Moreover, a recurrent dream is very important, as it is the intuitive voice of your subconscious saying to you, "Stop, look, and listen." The word *mountain* to her meant an insuperable obstacle. I suggested to her that she speak to her fiance about the dream and gain the assurance that there was nothing hidden that was not revealed to her and nothing covered that was not made known to her.

Accordingly, she flew down to Los Angeles to see her fiance, who met her at the airport. After a heart-to-heart talk, he finally told her, "I am a homosexual. I wanted to marry you so that my customers, who are very religious, would not suspect anything."

Her dream prevented her from experiencing what eventually would have been a great traumatic shock. You too can exercise the same or greater foresight through analyzing the recurrent happenings in your dreams.

The Reason for Her Dreams

This young lady had sensed something wrong for some months but could not put her finger on it. She prayed specifically, claiming that the infinite intelligence of her subconscious mind would reveal the answer and that it would be clearly shown to her.

The Bible says: *In a dream, in a vision of the night, when deep sleep falleth upon men, in slumberings upon the bed; Then he openeth the ears of men, and sealeth their instruction* (Job 33:15, 16).

There Are Many Types of Dreams

There are variegated types of dreams, some due to sexual frustration and repression, others due to mental and emotional turmoil, bodily malfunctioning, fears and religious taboos, reproduction and a recast of past events or of the activities of the day.

However, there are many dreams of a recurrent nature as well as of a precognitive significance wherein you see events before they happen. Many times you are given detailed instructions in the dream state as to what action to take.

How a Dream Revealed to a Woman the Man She Married

A young business woman had a dream in which she saw a young man—tall, fair, blue-eyed, and with blond hair. In the dream he proposed to her and she accepted. A few days later she met him when he entered the office where she worked to interview one of the attorneys who employed her. He invited her out and they shortly became fast friends. Two months later they were married.

Dreams similar to this one are quite frequent, as it is not at all uncommon for a man or woman to envisage ahead of time the person the dreamer will marry. It is possible to tap great intuitive powers by putting your dreams to work, as in this instance.

The Real Cause of This Woman's Prescience

This young woman had been praying and affirming every night for the ideal mate as follows: "I know that I am one with God now. In Him I live, move, and have my being. God is Life; this life is the life of all men and women. We are all sons and daughters of the one Father.

"I know and believe there is a man waiting to love and cherish me. I know I can contribute to his happiness and peace. He loves my ideals, and I love his ideals. He does not want to make me over; neither do I want to make him over. There are mutual love, freedom, and respect.

"There is one mind; I know him now in this mind. I unite with the qualities and attributes that I admire and want expressed by my husband. I am one with them in my mind. We know and love each other already in Divine Mind. I see the God in him; he sees the God in me. Having met him within, I must meet him in the without; for this is the law of my own mind.

"These words go forth and accomplish whereunto they are sent. I know it is now done, finished, and accomplished in God. Thank you, Father."

These truths which she affirmed found their way into her subconscious mind, and having identified herself with the qualities she admired in a man, her subconscious revealed to her the answer and a man who was the embodiment of her ideal was automatically attracted to her.

Extrasensory Perception Is Activated in Sleep

> *When thou goest, it shall lead thee; when thou sleepest, it shall keep thee; and when thou awakest, it shall talk with thee* (Proverbs 6:22).

In sleep your conscious mind is creatively joined to your subconscious mind. Many good people think that sleep is intended only for rest of the body, but nothing rests while you are asleep, as your subconscious and all the vital processes of your body, though slowed down considerably, continue to function. A restorative process sets in during sleep resulting in a feeling of well-being due to the fact that there is a restoration of physical energy. Another reason we go to sleep is to develop spiritually; therefore, it is of paramount importance that we avoid all discordant states prior to sleep. The Divinity that shapes our ends is all wise and has so arranged it that man is compelled to withdraw from the world of noise, which is not conducive to spiritual unfoldment.

Man is Divinely guided in sleep. Answers to many problems are given him in the sleep state. Formulas, inventive devices, poems, contents for many volumes, etc., are also given him in the dream state. The contents of many chapters in chemical textbooks and in the engineering laboratories of the world appeared in a dream, an answer to a request of the dreamer.

How to Invent and Discover Something New

You may have a vague or general idea of what you want to invent or discover and that is all. The technique is simple.

Learn all you can about it objectively and then in a passive and relaxed state, dwell on a mental picture of that which you wish to invent. Then turn over your mental picture to your subconscious, asking it to complete all details, and go to sleep. When you awaken, be sure to follow the "hunches" you receive. It sometimes comes as an inner feeling that the solution lies in a certain direction or in a certain group of facts. You will find that many times the entire formula or solution may appear in a dream. In such cases it is wise to have a pencil near you as you sleep so tha. when you awaken you may jot down the impressions that come to you in your dreams. You may be greatly surprised as to what has been given to you in your sleeping state.

Some say, "I never dream." We all dream. If you don't remember your dreams, suggest to your subconscious before you drop off to sleep two words. "I remember." It knows what you want to remember and will faithfully follow your instructions.

It is done unto you as you believe. Your dream state may be one of your most positive doorways to psychic perception.

POINTS TO REMEMBER

1. The Bible is replete with references to dreams, visions, and revelations given to man when he is sound asleep.

2. Dreams have been studied down through the ages, and in almost every culture, interpreters and expositors of dreams and visions of the night have been employed.

3. Dreams are dramatizations of your subconscious mind and may answer your problems symbolically or warn you of impending danger. Your future is in your subconscious mind now, based upon your subjective impressions, beliefs, and assumptions.

4. You mold, fashion, and create your own future based upon your habitual thinking and imagery. Your subconscious mind, which never sleeps, is constantly reproducing your mental impressions and acceptances.

5. Symbols are personal to each individual and may have a different meaning when appearing in the dreams of another. The interpretation must coincide with your inner feeling. In other words, it must make sense to you.

6. A woman seeking to know where money was hidden requested her subconscious mind to reveal the whereabouts of the money, and it responded in a dream, showing the location of the secret place and how to open the receptacle in the wall. The subconscious knows all and sees all.

7. A young lady, sensing something wrong about her fiance, requested her subconscious to reveal specifically the answer to her, which it did in the form of an extraordinarily high mountain between them in a dream. Intuitively, she understood what the mountain was (a formidable obstacle impossible to climb over) and asked her intended about it. He blurted out frankly that he was marrying her as a sort of front to set at rest the suspicions of his customers, who were very religious in an old-fashioned way. Her dream saved her from a great traumatic shock. Her fiance was a homosexual.

8. There are many types of dreams. For example, if you go to sleep very thirsty, you may find yourself in your dreams quaffing large amounts of water. Also, dreams may dramatize frustrations, fears, phobias, fixations, and complexes of all kinds. Furthermore, there are many recurrent dreams and precognitive dreams which reveal events before they

happen. Many answers are given to the most perplexing problems in dreams and visions of the night.

9. It is not unusual to envisage your future husband or wife in a dream. This occurs because you have been meditating on certain qualities you desire in your future spouse, and as soon as you have deposited these qualities in your subconscious mind, by thinking of them with interest, it gives you a preview of the man or woman who is the embodiment of your idea.

10. Extrasensory perception is activated in sleep. When you go to sleep, your conscious mind is creatively joined to your subconscious mind; the last waking concept you entertain prior to sleep is etched on your subconscious mind and the latter determines the way the answer or healing will take place.

11. Many times as you think of the answer prior to sleep you will find that the entire formula or solution may appear in a dream. It is done unto you as you believe.

9

How Your Psychic Mind Solves Problems Through Dream Impressions

I have observed with the passage of years that people in all walks of life are intensely fascinated by dreams. Our daily newspapers, periodicals, and magazines are continuously revealing the extensive research work being conducted by medical doctors, psychologists, and psychiatrists on the dream life of men and women, and they have demonstrated that practically without exception all people dream. This research work has demonstrated also that deprivation of needed sleep can bring on mental aberrations and even psychosis.

Nearly everyone today has heard of Freud, Jung, Adler, and many others. These men have written and lectured extensively on dreams, and their interpretations vary to a great degree. From time immemorial, men and women have been baffled and amazed by the dramatizations of the mind called dreams. Many of these dreams are of a precognitive nature and transcend time and space.

The Television Set of His Mind Revealed the Answer

A young college student told me recently that he looks at the "television" in his mind every night. He refers to his dreams as his mental television. He had been ill for a couple of weeks and had missed several important lectures but was scheduled nevertheless to take an examination the day after his return to his studies. The night prior to the examination, he instructed his subconscious as follows: "Infinite Intelligence, you are all-wise. Reveal to me everything I need to know about this examination tomorrow morning. I accept the answer now." He then calmly went off to the deep of sleep. That night he saw clearly all the questions on his mental TV set and immediately thereafter got up and studied the answers from his textbook. This happens frequently to this young man, who definitely believes that the wisdom of his subconscious mind is guiding him in all his studies.

How Her Dream Saved Her Life

While writing this chapter, I was interrupted by a long distance call from a member of our organization who was in London, England at that time. The following is the gist of what she said: "I had to phone you. Last night you appeared to me in my dream and warned me under no circumstances to go to Nottingham by car as I had arranged. You instructed me to go by train. I had arranged to go with my two cousins in their car, but I cancelled the trip as you suggested. I was shocked to learn a short time later that my two cousins had experienced a serious accident on the road and were badly injured."

Her Special Prayer Program

Prior to this young woman's departure for Europe, I had given her the following prayer with the instructions that she was to busy her mind with the simple truths therein contained: "I travel under God's guidance at all times. I send my messengers called Divine love, peace, harmony, and right action before me to make straight, beautiful, joyous, and happy my way, knowing that with mine eyes stayed on God, there is no evil on my pathway.

"Whilst riding in a car, train, bus, airplane, or whatever means of conveyance I use, God's love surrounds me. The invisible armor of God is always around me. The spirit of God is upon me, making all roads a highway for my God. It is wonderful!"

The Reason for Her Dream

Self-preservation is the first law of life, and your subconscious always seeks to guard and preserve you from harm of every kind. The prayer she was using was etched on her subconscious mind, which activated its clairvoyant powers. Undoubtedly it knew that if she had traveled by motor car to Nottingham, she would have had an accident; therefore, it projected a picture of her minister and dramatized the words of warning which her subconscious knew she would heed and obey. My appearance in her dream was simply a symbol of the truth of the message imparted to her in her dream.

She Could Not Take That Motor Trip

It is important to remember that harmony and discord do not dwell together; therefore, she could not be in a car that collided with another, as she had claimed Divine love and harmony go before her, making straight, joyous, and peaceful her journey.

He Said, "I Never Dream"

The subconscious mind is ever awake even during the deepest rest of the body, and it is always active. A young man who has been attending my lectures imagined that his profound sleep was dreamless, since he did not recall his dreams on awakening. I suggested to him that on the moment of awakening he suggest to himself, "I remember," and to his surprise and pleasure, the dream unfolded itself completely and even answered a problem for him which had perplexed him for some time.

Her Dream Saved Her from a Serious Operation

A girl whom we shall call Louise was informed by her foot surgeon that it was necessary to operate on her left foot to bring about a healing, and that this would necessitate having her leg in a cast as well as using crutches for two months or more. She prayed that the infinite intelligence of her subconscious mind would guide and direct her to come to the right decision. She turned this request over to her subconscious mind every night, and at the end of the fourth night, she saw a chiropractic doctor, a friend of the family, who in the dream state pointed to Hexagram 35 in *The I Ching,** which said, "Progress." The next day she went to visit him, and on examining the foot, he advised her that he could bring about perfect alignment and adjustment by manipulation and exercise, which she would have to practice; and a perfect healing followed.

The Reason Her Subconscious Selected the Hexagram

The subconscious usually speaks and reveals answers symbolically. Louise, having taken two classes on *The I Ching* with the writer, became absorbed and engrossed with its scientific and metaphysical approach to life and, undoubtedly, her subconscious knew she would follow the directions of the hexagram. It spoke literally to her when it revealed the doctor she should see for the healing of her foot.

_____

The I Ching, or Book of Changes, Wilhelm/Baynes Edition, Bollingen Series XIX (New Jersey: Princeton University Press, 1950).

**An Artist Attributes Her Success to
Entering the Subjective State at Will**

In visiting the home of an artist recently, I was told that she could enter the subjective state at will by simply closing her eyes, immobilizing her attention, and requesting her subconscious to give her beautiful mental pictures in detail and color. She is aware that her subconscious mind is amenable to her suggestions and that her visions of beauty are evoked by her own volition. All she has to do is to paint the corresponding colors upon the canvas. She has discovered the gold mine within herself and knows how to mine the beauties and glories within.

He Listened to the Inner Monitor and Saved His Life

On a recent visit to Honolulu, I called on an old friend whose Hawaiian mother told him when he was very young: "Claim every day of your life that the spell of God is always around you and that you bear a charmed life." He practices this great truth regularly and systematically, and naturally his subconscious mind responds. It responds by corresponding.

One night, as he was within a block of his home, he heard this inner voice of intuition say clearly to him, "Don't enter your home. Call the police." He said the words were clear and distinct. He phoned the police and told them thieves were ransacking his home. (He felt this intuitively.) The police arrived within minutes and caught the two burglars, who were armed with pistols and were highly dangerous. They were quickly arrested. One of the detectives told my friend later that had he entered his home and surprised the burglars, they would undoubtedly have shot him, which they had done previously to others under similar circumstances.

Our boasted God-like *reason* does not have all the answers to our daily problems; it is of the earth—earthly. Our reasoning faculty is the noblest attribute of our conscious mind, but it is essentially finite and *primarily for the three-dimensional world.* It is our daily guide in the walks of our objective life and physical environment, but *your subconscious mind is one with infinite intelligence and boundless wisdom and is untrammeled by the objective senses, physical form, and earthly conditions,* and is unimpeded by the processes of finite reasoning. Your subconscious imbibes the truth and the answers to your problems from the eternal source.

POINTS TO REMEMBER

1. People in all walks of life are fascinated by dreams. Practically every high school boy is familiar with the names of Freud, Adler, and Jung, who have written extensively on dreams and whose interpretations vary greatly. Many dreams are of a precognitive nature and are of profound importance to you.
2. A young college student refers to his dreams as a "TV set" in his mind. By repeated affirmations to his subconscious mind, he has succeeded in having it respond to him with the questions to be propounded to him on his examination.
3. A girl travelling in Europe reiterated a special prayer of protection by sending thought messengers of Divine love, peace, harmony, and right action before her, and her subconscious responded by protecting her against a possible fatal accident.
4. Your subconscious may project the symbolic image of your minister to you in a dream state in order that you may be alerted to the seriousness of the warning when it refers to your self-preservation. The ways of your subconscious are past finding out.
5. Everyone dreams. If you say, "I never dream," all you have to do when you awaken is say to yourself one word: "Remember," and the important dreams

will come in perfect sequence into your conscious, reasoning mind.

6. If you are a student of the Bible or of *The I Ching*, it is quite possible that your subconscious may project a hexagram in answer to your request and by following the diagnosis and prognosis of the hexagram, you have the answer. All the allegories and symbols of the Bible come from illumined men who tapped the marvelous powers of their subjective psychic minds.

7. A great artist stills her mind and immobilizes her attention, and in a quiet, passive, psychic, and receptive state, requests her psychic mind to give her visions of beauty and grandeur, which she depicts on her canvas. She requests that these pictures be given in detail and in color, and her subconscious responds accordingly. She refers to her subconscious as the gold mine within her.

8. A man in Honolulu, when a boy, was given by his mother a benediction to affirm every day, such as: "The spell of God is always around me and I bear a charmed life." His subconscious spoke to him by a clear inner voice, which said, "Don't enter your home. Call the police." He followed the instructions and discovered that he was saved from what the detectives asserted would be certain death. The wisdom of your subconscious, when called upon and trusted, never fails.

10

Extrasensory Perception
and Your Subconscious

Your subconscious mind expresses what is impressed upon it. Many so-called strange occurrences, projections, and voices are nothing but subjective manifestations. The ghosts we fear are those that walk the gloomy galleries of our minds.

Your Subconscious Is an Open Book

To the intuitive, psychic, or sensitive person with clairvoyant powers, your subconscious is an open book. It is possible for a good psychic to reveal past experiences as well as future events, which are already present in your subconscious. He could possibly be 90 percent or more accurate. You might get a different reading from another psychic or sensitive. This would be due to the fact that what each one sees is filtered through his own mentality and the interpretation may be somewhat different.

The thoughts, plans, and experiences of man can also be read by interpreting a deck of cards, by gazing into a crystal ball, or by examining the convolutions of some sand arrangements as well as other devices. From time immemorial man has attributed certain values to numbers, cards, and other symbols. Since man nas assigned authority and power to these things, they must confirm his beliefs symbolically. By getting into a partly subjective or passive state, it is possible to reveal the contents of the subjective mind of a person. The cards, or marks on the sand, or the moving pictures in the crystal ball serve as an alphabet of your subconscious mind, and when pieced together by the psychic, speak in a language understood by you.

Your Character Can Be Delineated

Perhaps you have been surprised sometimes that when an astrologer, numerologist, or card reader read your character, you agreed with the delineation and said to yourself that it was very accurate. Remember, however, that your disposition, tendencies, predilections, early training, and indoctrination are registered and embodied in your subconscious mind. If a person is highly intuitive, he simply tunes in with your subconscious mind and reveals your characteristics to your conscious mind. Actually, you had already informed the sensitive of everything before she told you anything. All she did was to tune in, or get in rapport with your subconscious mind.

How She Neutralized the Negative
Prediction of an Accident

I was visited by a young woman who was emotionally distraught over a prediction of a palmist that she would have a serious accident on or near her 21st birthday. She had accepted the suggestion and consequently was afraid to travel by auto, train, or plane. She was living in perpetual fear and had impressed her subconscious with the belief in an accident. Having actuated it with fear, it would undoubtedly have come to pass had she not learned how to neutralize the accepted negative thought.

How She Prayed and Affirmed in a Definite Manner

"Wherever I go—by bus, foot, automobile, train, or plane, or whatever means of conveyance I use—I know, believe, and accept the truth that Divine love goes before me making joyous, glorious, and happy my way. I know that Infinite Intelligence guides and directs me at all times and I am always in the sacred circle of God's eternal love. The whole armor of God enfolds me at all times, and all my ways and travels are controlled by God and by God alone. God controls all travel in the heavens above and on the earth beneath, making all my journeys a highway for God."

Her Technique for Eradicating the Negative Prediction

She affirmed these truths every morning, afternoon, and night, knowing that these spiritual vibrations would obliterate and expunge from her subconscious mind the negative suggestion which was charged with fear. She is now 23 years of age, and she experienced the happiest day of her life on her 21st birthday. She got married to a childhood friend, and they are extremely happy. Paul says, *Whether there be prophecies, they shall fail.* (I Cor. 13:8).

How to Learn to Shape and Mold Your Own Destiny

Your thought and feeling create your destiny. *All things, whatsoever ye shall ask in prayer, believing, ye shall receive* (Matthew 21:22). To believe something is to accept it as true. What you decide to be true with your conscious mind, you will experience with your subconscious mind. Your subconscious is the major operation of your life. You might look upon your mind somewhat like an iceberg: 90 percent of it is below water. Likewise, you are over 90 percent controlled by your subconscious mind's assumptions, convictions, and conditioning. Your subconscious beliefs dictate, control, and manipulate all your conscious actions. Begin now to believe, claim, feel, and know that God is guiding you in all ways, that Divine right action governs you at all times, that God is prospering you in all ways, and that you are inspired from On High. As you accept these truths with your conscious mind, your subconscious will bring all these to pass and you will discover that all your ways are pleasantness and all your paths are peace.

How You Can Overcome the Law of Averages

Your subconscious mind is amenable to control and direction by your conscious mind. If you do not direct your subconscious mind according to universal principles and eternal verities, you will live according to the law of averages, which means you will be subject to the thinking of the masses, and this, as you know, is mostly negative. Millions of people are living lives of mediocrity, lack, and limitation of all kinds because they don't direct their subconscious mind properly. They fail to impregnate it with the thoughts of harmony, peace, joy, abundance, security, and right action. Your subconscious mind reproduces 24 hours a day your habitual thinking. Begin now to activate your conscious mind spiritually and your subconscious will do the rest.

When your conscious mind completely accepts a creative idea and turns it over to your subconscious with conviction, the law of your subconscious brings it to pass in your experience. Man is mind, and evermore he takes the tool of thought and chooses what he wills, bringing forth a thousand joys or a thousand ills.

How to Predict a Wonderful Life for Yourself

There is absolutely no one who can predict with accuracy for you if you think from the standpoint of principle. The Divine Intelligence knows what to do and how to do it. It responds to your habitual thinking; therefore, you are always predicting the future for yourself. As your thoughts are spiritual, noble, lofty, and God-like, you see the fallacy of fear of the unknown and belief in evil. Since you are a scientific thinker, your prophecy for yourself is harmony, health, peace, and all the blessings of life. You are the master of your fate and the captain of your soul.

Learn to walk the earth unmoved, unchallenged, and unshaken in the conviction that there is nothing too good to be true and nothing too wonderful to last, for the goodness, riches, harmony, and glories of God are the same yesterday, today, and forever.

How an Indian Boy Stopped the Flow of Blood

In a book called *This Is It,* published by the writer in 1944 (now out of print for many years), I wrote about an experience I had had about 40 years ago with an Indian boy. He could not read or write, yet he possessed the ability to stop the flow of arterial blood, which flows freely, by closing his eyes and saying, "Stop it." When he opened his eyes, the bleeding had ceased. He believed that his prayer would always be answered, and even though others mocked, he never failed.

How did this so-called ignorant boy acquire this ability? His explanation was as follows: As far back as he could remember, his father had told him that the power to staunch blood was a tradition in the family and was handed down from father to son. The first-born in the family had the gift, but none of the other members, brothers or sisters, possessed this power.

The boy grew up in this belief and fully accepted the fact that he could stop the flow of blood. If he saw it, he closed his eyes to it and issued the command, which was always obeyed. He really did not know how or why it should stop. He knew nothing about the subconscious mind or its powers. The reason the blood stopped flowing was that *he believed.* (He stated that while at home in Canada he frequently was called upon to stop cases of hemorrhaging.)

Why He Had to Be Present to Heal

A very peculiar thing about this healing capacity was that he believed that he had to be present and see the blood flow, and so he could not heal anyone at a distance. This was a belief implanted in his subconscious mind at an early age, and he accepted it as a part of the tradition of his tribe and family.

The Bible says: *For as the heavens are higher than the earth, so are my ways* (answers from the subconscious) *higher than your ways.* (Isaiah 55:9).

POINTS TO REMEMBER

1. Your subconscious mind expresses on the screen of space whatever you impress upon it, whether it be good or bad.

2. When a good psychic, medium, or clairvoyant gets into a passive, psychic state, he is *en rapport* with your subconscious mind and can tap its secrets, either through vivid mental pictures dramatized in his mind's eye or by intuitive impressions. Oftentimes your experiences may appear like a television series in his mind.

3. Your dispositions, heredity, leanings, tendencies, and temperament can be subjectively felt by a good astrologer, numerologist, or card reader, provided they are really intuitive and deeply psychic. This is why your character can be delineated even by a person who never heard of astrology or numerology, or at least one who knows nothing about the

subject. Cards, astrological charts, crystal balls, numbers, etc., are only symbols and are to the interpretation of your conscious mind a sort of alphabet of your deeper mind.

4. You can neutralize a negative prediction by contemplating the truths of God and thinking constructively from the standpoint of principle and eternal verities. The lower is always subject to the higher; therefore, the negative, fearful thoughts are dissipated and dissolved by your spiritual thoughts.

5. When you travel, you can build up an immunity to accidents of all kinds by contemplating regularly and systematically that Divine love goes before you making straight, glorious, and joyous your way. Keep on affirming that God's love and the whole armor of God surround you. After a while, you will impregnate your subconscious and become completely immunized and God-intoxicated.

6. Your thought and feeling create your destiny. What you decide is true in your conscious mind, your subconscious will produce. This is why you mold, fashion, and shape your future. Your subconscious is reproducing your habitual thinking 24 hours a day.

7. You can rise above the law of averages, which applies to the mass thinking of three billion people in this world. Think on whatsoever is true, noble, lofty, and God-like, and you become what you contemplate.

8. The Divine Intelligence in you knows what to do and how to do it. When you call upon it, you receive an answer. You can predict for yourself harmony, health, peace, joy, abundance, and security by thinking on these truths with interest. You will discover that your future is your present thinking made manifest.

9. A traditional belief handed down from father to son is accepted by the impressionable mind of the boy, and it is done unto him as he believes. Believing that the power to stop the flow of arterial blood is a Divine gift, the decree of the Indian boy gets results at once. The law of life is the law of belief.

11

The Dynamic Power of
Psychic Thought

The Bible says: *For as he thinketh in his heart* (subconscious mind), *so is he* (Proverbs 23:7). *In the beginning was the word, and the word was with God, and the word was God* (John 1:1). Your word is a thought expressed, and the Bible says the word was God, meaning your thought is creative, for there is only Creative Power—Spirit—and the function of Spirit is thought.

It is best you have a healthy regard and respect for your thought. The degree of your happiness, peace, prosperity, and success is determined by your habitual thinking. Your subconscious mind is constantly reproducing your conscious mind's thinking and imagery. Thoughts are things, and your thought has its own mathematics and mechanics of expression. When you reflect on thought, you are releasing the creative power of God, or infinite intelligence, into action. Emerson said: "Man is what he thinks all day long."

How He Proved the Power of Thought

Dr. Arthur Thomas, Minister of the Church of Religious

Science in Reno, Nevada, gave me permission to write this about him. Arthur had been a lieutenant in the British Navy at one time, and more recently had been in the wholesale business as well as in real estate in Los Angeles. About eight years ago, however, he started attending my lectures on Sunday mornings. He said, "I realized suddenly my thought was the only creative power of which I was aware, and I was going to create what I really wanted."

Consequently, he began to affirm to himself frequently: "I am a minister now. I am teaching the truths of life to people." Every night he would imagine he was expatiating on the great truths to a wonderful group of men and women in a church. He continued to think along these lines for a month or so when he decided to take the ministerial course at the Institute of Religious Science, confident of the end result, as he had already imagined and felt as true the reality of creative thinking.

He passed all tests and examinations in Divine order and was offered the church immediately after finishing his seminary course. He is now doing exactly what he decreed mentally. He knew that his subconscious mind would respond mathematically and accurately according to his thinking processes.

Get Acquainted with the Most Powerful Force in the Universe

Thought is the most powerful force in the universe. Your word is a thought expressed. If you are in a position of authority, your thought or word can direct how missiles, nuclear energy, dynamite or thermonuclear weapons are to be used. Your thought determines how electricity is to be used. Likewise, your thought directs the operation of your life. Your subconscious mind could be likened to an iceberg—90 percent of it is below the surface. It is your subconscious mind that does the work according to the orders given it by your conscious mind. What you think with your conscious mind you produce with your subconscious.

She Discovered the Wonders of Right Thinking

Dr. Elsie McCoy of Beverly Hills, who has given me permission to write on the following events, shows clearly what constructive thinking according to principle will accomplish. She has studied extensively in Europe and Asia and in her early days was engaged to a prominent surgeon. They were separated by over 1,000 miles, however, due to their different assignments.

Ever since she was 18 years of age, she has made it a habit to affirm frequently during the day: "Only Divine right action takes place in my life, and whatever I need to know is revealed to me instantly by the infinite intelligence within me." Her gradual reiteration of these truths caused them to reach the subconscious mind, which responded accordingly. One night while she was sound asleep, she saw and heard clearly in a vivid dream her fiance in Chicago talking to a nurse and, in addition, dating her for a week-end, saying to her, "You know, I'm engaged, but she is 1,000 miles away and knows nothing about it."

Dr. McCoy phoned him the next day and told him about the silly and foolish dream she had had and laughed about it. He was furious and accused her of having employed detectives and of spying upon him. With that she dissolved the engagement, and subsequent events showed the wisdom of her subconscious in protecting her from what would undoubtedly have been a tragic marriage.

Her right thinking activated her subconscious mind, which revealed to her what she should know before she got married.

A Famous Actor Gets an Amazing Answer
Through the Subconscious of Another

Dr. Olive Gaze, an associate of mine, authorized me to
write about the remarkable way the subconscious mind of
her mother, Josephine Wyndham, responded to the questions
propounded to her by the late Norman Trevor, a distinguished actor. Dr. Gaze said that he had a perplexing problem
and asked her mother if she could reveal the answer to him.
Josephine Wyndham was highly intuitive.

She began to think quietly and feelingly for a few
minutes, "Right answer." Her subconscious took over and
controlled her right hand. She began to write, completing
about two pages. When she looked at it, she could not read a
word of her own writing; neither could her daughter, the
present Dr. Olive Gaze.

She gave the written material to Norman Trevor, and he
read it with ease and alacrity. It was written in Hindustani,
which he understood perfectly, having lived in India for
many years. The message was a full and complete answer to
his perplexing problem. They were all amazed at the wonders
of right thinking and the response of the subconscious mind.

My explanation of this is that Josephine Wyndham,
being very intuitive, got into a very relaxed, quiet, passive,
psychic, receptive state of mind, which brings about an
outcropping of the subconscious and a partial submergence
of the conscious mind. In this state, she was *en rapport* with
his subconscious mind, and she tapped the contents of his
subconscious, including the language of Hindustani. Since the
nature of the subconscious is compulsive, it took control of
her hand and wrote in a language and in a way which would
be convincing, and which he would believe. The ways of the
subconscious are past understanding.

How She Activated Her Subconscious Mind

Mrs. Louise Barrows told me that on New Year's Eve,

1970, one of the requests she turned over to her subconscious mind was that she would take a trip to Europe with her two teenage boys in Divine order. She wrote it as follows: "My two boys and I are going to Europe in July this summer, 1970, in Divine order. I accept this idea now in my conscious mind, and my subconscious brings it to pass."

In February of 1970 a close relative asked her if she would like to take a European holiday to Switzerland, Germany, Italy, etc., with her two sons, and she accepted; all expenses of the trip had already been paid to the travel agency by her relative. Her subconscious mind knew how to bring it to pass, and it acted on the mind of the wealthy relative, compelling him to make the offer. In other words, he was the instrument through which the money and the facilities manifested. Her spiritual thinking was a command to her subconscious to bring her request to pass.

How to Think (Pray) Successfully

Your thought is your prayer. When your conscious mind deliberately accepts a creative idea or plan and turns it over to the subconscious with confidence, the intelligence of your subconscious brings it to pass in your experience. Your subconscious mind acts as a law and produces with mathematical exactitude the equivalent of your idea in your experience.

Right Thinking Enables Her to Lose Forty Pounds

A young lady wrote me from Wichita, Kansas, saying she had been reading *The Power of Your Subconscious Mind** and decided to follow her doctor's instructions and lose 40 pounds. She stated that she had gone on many diet regimens, and took off weight only to put it on again.

---

*Dr. Joseph Murphy, *The Power of Your Subconscious Mind* (Englewood Cliffs, N.J.: Prentice-Hall, Inc., 1963).

However, following the advice given in the book, prior to sleep every night she began to think right and to convey the right command to her subconscious mind. Her right thinking was as follows: "I weigh 118 pounds in Divine order. The infinite intelligence of my subconscious mind accepts this request and acts accordingly. I sleep in peace and Divine right action governs me."

After a week or so, she discovered that she had lost all desire for the amylaceous foods and fatty substances which she previously craved and thus had no trouble losing the required weight. Before this, she had been forcing herself to follow the strict diet, while at the same time lusting after ice cream, apple pie, and assorted sweets.

Anyone who says, "I can't lose weight" is actually saying, "I don't want to lose weight." All you have to do is to come to a clear-cut decision in your conscious mind, and your subconscious will do the rest. You will discover you will lose all desire for those foods that contribute to your obesity.

You Are the Only Thinker in Your Universe

You have the privilege of selecting any constructive idea; nourish it and sustain it, knowing that there is a response from your subconscious mind. The wisdom of your subconscious will work out the idea which you have selected in its own unique way.

The Power of Thought on Your Body

You have observed the effect of fear on your pulse, heart beat, etc. Shame brings a flush to the cheek and anger and rage blanch the skin. The hair of many young men has turned white when they were exposed to a harrowing experience. News of a sudden death of a loved one has brought on psychological blindness and deafness. Worry interferes with digestion and may bring on ulcers, colitis, and other malfunctions and diseases. Our newspapers and periodicals are pointing out daily the ravages of hate, envy, jealousy, and strain on the body, such as anemia, high blood pressure, cardiac disorders, and even cancer.

Begin to Use the Creative Power Wisely

Your consciousness is the only creative power in your life. Your consciousness represents what you think, feel, believe, and give mental consent to. This is the cause of all your experiences, conditions, circumstances, and events in your life. Do not make the external world a cause; it is an effect.

Refuse definitely, positively, and absolutely to give power to externals, such as the winds, waves, weather, sun, snow, stars, or any created thing. The scientific thinker never makes an effect a cause; therefore, he is no longer hypnotized by the world and its beliefs. The creator is greater than his creation. The thinker is greater than his thoughts, and the artist is greater than his art. Think good and good follows; think negatively and negation follows.

He Asked the Real Meaning of Thought and Thinking

At a lecture I held last year in Las Vegas, a man asked the question: "What is thought and thinking, and what is new about it?" I explained to him that thinking means comparing; i.e., comparing one thing with another, one proposition with another. If the mental instrument can say only "yes," comparison is not possible. You have a choice between two things—to one of them you say "yes," to the other "no." When you ask "why?" you are seeking a reason. All reasoning involves selecting this and rejecting that, and it would be impossible to select or reject unless your mind had the power of affirmation and rejection.

Most people don't really think. We are thinking when our minds are dedicated to the eternal truths of God, when we reject all fear and contemplate the reality of our desire, knowing there is an Almighty Power which responds to our thinking and which will bring it to pass. You are truly thinking when you reason things out in your mind, rejecting all negative concepts as unfit for the house of God, and feasting on the reality of the Divine solution, while knowing that a subjective wisdom responds to your creative thought when you are free from fear.

This seemed to satisfy him, and he said, "I never knew what thought was until now." Man is mind, and evermore he takes the tool of thought and brings forth a thousand joys or a thousand ills.

POINTS TO REMEMBER

1. Your psychic thought is creative. When you think the thought, you release the latent power within you. Every thought tends to manifest itself.

2. By reiterating a certain thought pattern in your conscious mind, your subconscious receives it and decides in its own way how to bring it to pass. Your mental image is a thought-pattern in your mind, and by regularly and systematically imagining yourself doing what you love to do, your subconscious develops that mental image in the dark house of your mind and brings it to pass.

3. Your thought is the most powerful force in the world. A word is a thought expressed. Therefore, man can determine how atomic, nuclear, and electrical energies and powers are to be used. Man is the master, and is in control. He must decide how he is going to use the powers available to him.

4. When you affirm, "Whatever I need to know is revealed to me instantly," your psychic mind will protect you from making errors or mistakes. A young doctor who impregnated her subconscious

mind with this truth saw in a dream her fiance's relationship with another woman. She cancelled the proposed marriage and discovered she was Divinely protected from making a tragic mistake.

5. There are many gifted people called psychic automatists.

6. A mother of two teenage boys wrote out a request on New Year's Eve that psychic intelligence would reveal the perfect way for her to take her two sons to Europe during July. A wealthy relative voluntarily paid all expenses for an extended vacation for all of them in Europe.

7. Your thoughts of fear, worry, anxiety and anger are quite noticeable in your face, eyes, pulse, blood pressure, or the blanching of your skin. Worry, hate, jealousy, and hostility are behind a host of maladies. Your psychic thought is creative.

8. Consciousness is the only creative power. Your consciousness means the way you think, feel, believe, and what you give mental consent to. Think good and good follows through your psychic perception.

9. To think is to compare, i.e., to choose one thing in preference to another. Your mental instrument can say "yes" or "no." Your mind has the power of affirmation and rejection. You are truly thinking when your thoughts conform to the eternal verities. Emerson said, "You are what you think all day long."

12

How to Use Secrets
of Extrasensory Perception
in Solving Problems

A certain woman (whom we shall call Mrs. Jones) was before a judge who was about to render a verdict in her case. She was very nervous, distraught, and worried. Her stepdaughters were contesting their father's will and were very bitter toward her. She also said that the judge didn't seem very sympathetic, even though her husband had willed only 50 percent of his estate to her.

At my suggestion, she followed this technique of prayer: "I know that Infinite Intelligence guides and directs my attorney, the judge, and all concerned in this case. I realize and know that the Divine law of harmony reigns supreme and that which was bequeathed to me comes to me in Divine law and order." She knew that by practicing these truths, she would activate these principles of truth resident in her subconscious psychic mind.

Her Visualization Technique

She said to herself, "The architect visualizes the skyscraper; he sees it as he want it to be. His mental image becomes a mold from which the building will finally emerge." Accordingly, she affirmed: "The judge is absolutely honest. God thinks, speaks, and acts through him, and his decision is based on Divine right action." She pictured the judge announcing his decision, saying: "My decision is just and eminently fair and is in accordance with the provision of the will and the intent of the deceased."

She visualized the judge, saying this over and over again until her mind became saturated with the truth of what she affirmed. Undoubtedly this same truth was resurrected in the subconscious mind of the judge, who made a decision exactly as she had decreed, which was according to the provisions of her husband's will and his true intention. By her recognition and appreciation of the principle of right action, the avarice and envy of her stepdaughters were brought to naught. You too can help solve your problems satisfactorily by proceeding as Mrs. Jones did.

How Extrasensory Perception
Cured His Abnormal Jealousy

A salesman confided to me that he was never certain about his wife, Mary, when he was away. She was extremely attractive, young, and beautiful. During his frequent trips to many cities in the territory allocated to him, he lived in constant fear that he would lose her or that she would become enamored with some young man in the neighborhood. He would phone her four or five times a day, which disturbed her, as she knew the reasons for his frequent phone calls.

I explained to him that basically and fundamentally his jealousy was due to a sense of insecurity and a feeling of inferiority within himself.

The Healing Technique He Employed

When away from home, he would still his mind two or

three times a day, get quiet inside, and relax his body. Then he would imagine Mary right in front of him, and he would affirm: "Divine love unites us," and "I love you sincerely." She would reply, "I love you—you are the only one." He would hear her say these words to him regularly and feelingly. Whenever the urge came to him to call in order to check up on her, he would silently affirm: "Divine love unites us. I love her and she loves me, also."

He felt the reality of these words in his heart, and as he drove along the road he could hear Mary's voice, the texture and tone of which he knew very well, ring in his ears, saying "I love you." After a week or so of practicing this technique, he discovered that love really casts out fear and jealousy.

How Tom Overcame His Nightmares

A man (we shall call him Tom) phoned me relative to the frightful nightmares he had experienced every night for over a week. He wanted to know how to overcome this condition. He said that he knew the agent in the dream is always the dreamer himself, be he the attacker or the attacked. He was being torn to pieces by fierce wild animals in his sleep, and at other times in the night, viciously beaten by thugs and left for dead.

I explained to him that undoubtedly his nightmares were punishments for his feeling of guilt, and dramatized in symbolic form by ferocious beasts clawing and attacking him. He admitted that being pursued, overpowered, and destroyed by animals and thugs and his awakening perspiring with fear and foreboding of some imminent disaster was due to his aggressive hatred toward a woman with whom he was in love and who had jilted him for another man.

His nightmares were really the fires of hatred, hostility, and suppressed rage and could be called the eruption of his conscience. His insight and perception into his own condition transcended his five-sense knowledge.

The Technique and Formula He Used
to Banish His Frightful Nightmares

At my suggestion, he decided to lie flat on his back prior to sleep and visualize his former girl friend and her husband as radiant, happy, joyous, and free. He consciously projected love, harmony, peace, and goodwill to both of them, saying out loud: "These God-like vibrations go forth from me now and are resurrected subjectively in the hearts of both of them. There is no time or space in the subconscious mind, and I know that what I really feel and am broadcasting now is lodged deeply in the hearts of my former girl friend and her husband. I sleep in peace and God gives me joy and happiness, and God's love fills my soul."

He practiced this technique for about ten minutes, and that night he slept peacefully and has had no trouble since then. His subconscious was controlled by his conscious mind. Feeding his subconscious with life-giving patterns, he wiped out the negative patterns. Love casts out fear.

Don't Ignore Your Dreams

Everyone dreams, though many people—usually the happy, joyous, and free—are unaware that they do dream. Many wish to ignore their dreams because their dreams are actually revealing subconscious states of mind which they don't want to be reminded of; therefore, they tend to suppress their hostilities and resentments. In sleep, the subconscious takes over and dramatizes its contents and protests to the conscious, sleeping mind that it should stop polluting its subconscious with negative and destructive mental poisons.

It is also true that while we sleep our dreams help us considerably in eradicating excess tension and anxiety. This happens whether we recall the fact we were dreaming or not. The subconscious is all-wise and it works off our pent-up emotions during sleep.

Nightmares and insomnia are amenable to control by the illumined conscious mind. Fill your conscious mind with the truths of God and reiterate these truths prior to sleep. Since your subconscious mind is subject to the conscious mind, you will sleep in peace and wake in joy.

How Ann's Extrasensory Powers Harmonized the Situation with Her Associate

A young supervisor (we shall call her Ann) was working in an office employing 20 girls. One of the girls, whom we shall call Lucy, was extremely hostile to her and in many subtle ways placed difficulties in her path. Furthermore, Lucy accused Ann of discriminating against her, pointing out that she was entitled to promotions and that her talents were not appreciated nor given recognition. Ann did not want to recommend her dismissal, as Lucy, though very difficult to handle, was capable in her work. Moreover, Ann didn't want her to begin to complain to the management that she was being discriminated against when, in reality, she was not.

How Ann Overcame the Hurdle

At my suggestion, one morning Ann sat down in her office, quieted her mind, and read the 91st Psalm while affirming deeply and lovingly: "I am filled with the free-flowing love of God. My whole being is saturated with Divine love. I fully and freely forgive Lucy. The Spirit in me talks to the Spirit in Lucy and there are harmony, love, and understanding between us. Whenever I see Lucy, or whenever she speaks to me, I surround her with a circle of light and love.

Ann practiced this technique during the day for about four days, and at the end of this time Lucy apologized to her for the way she was acting and promised complete cooperation in the future. Ann's benediction and prayers had actually engulfed the soul of Lucy and they became great friends. What Ann projected or "broadcast" came back to her. As you send out love and goodwill, so will it return to you. Action and reaction are equal.

How a Young Lady Used Extrasensory Perception to Find Her Long-Lost Father

A few weeks ago I visited Ulu Maui Village in Hawaii. Here the villagers stage lively demonstrations of poi-pounding, old time hulas, lei-making, quilt weaving, and other traditional rites, concepts, and arts. This village offers intriguing displays of ancient *tapas,* Hawaiian and Pacific artifacts. It is said: "You haven't seen Hawaii until you've seen Ulu Maui." I had a superb Hawaiian luncheon served with exotic South Seas concoctions. Chatting with a young lady at the next table, I told her I was writing a book entitled *Let Psychic Perception Work for You* and was looking for some material in Hawaii, the island of mystery, and from the Kahuna (native priest).

She said, "You can use my story; it is very vivid and real." The following is the gist of her experience. Her father had deserted her mother when my luncheon companion was two years old; it seems they had quarreled a lot. The father had given the mother $25,000 for the care and education of the child. When the child had grown up and graduated from the University of Hawaii, where she majored in psychology, she decided to use the powers of her mind to locate her father, whom she had an intense desire to meet and to know.

How Her Awareness of Her Astral Body Helped Her

She said, "I know I possess a fourth-dimensional, subtle body, which some call the astral body, as I have found myself out of my body frequently and on foreign shores." She pointed out that her astral body fitted exactly the contours of her physical body.

One night prior to sleep she instructed her subconscious mind in the following manner: "You know where my father is. I know you can make me appear before him in person, whether he is asleep or awake, wherever he is. Your guiding intelligence will now find him, as you are my inner radar. There is a love bond between my father and myself. He hungers to meet me and I hunger to meet him. This is my command to you, and now I go to sleep in peace." These words are the essence of the instructions she communicated to her subconscious mind.

"Immediately after going to sleep, I found myself in a hotel room in Sydney, Australia," she said. "I had a body exactly the same as the one lying in bed in Honolulu, and there I saw my father putting on his coat getting ready to go to work. He seemed startled and frightened, and I said to him, 'Dad, I'm Lisa (not her real name), your daughter. I love you. Come back to us.' He seemed speechless and dumbfounded, and all I remember is that he said, 'I will.' Then I found myself back in my three-dimensional body on the bed in my home in Honolulu."

The Interesting Sequel to Her Astral Travel

Lisa had a perfect memory of what had happened while she was asleep. When she awakened in the morning, she told her mother where her father was staying in Sydney. She wrote to him there and told him about her astral visit, and she received a reply by airmail, saying he had experienced an apparition of a beautiful young lady who appeared to him in his bedroom saying she was his daughter, and he said that he was coming back to Honolulu. They had a joyous reunion and her mother welcomed her long-lost husband with open arms.

How She Functioned Outside Her Body

Prior to sleep, Lisa decreed to her subconscious that the guiding principle in her subconscious mind would lead her to her father, and it projected her personality, which was immediately presented to her father in her astral body. This happened almost instantaneously, inasmuch as she was asleep by the clock for less than five minutes. She had full use of her faculties; she was consciously aware of the hotel, its address, the furniture in the room where her father was; and she was able to communicate to him and move ponderable objects. Also, she had visual, auditory, and tactile capacities.

In other words, she proved to herself that she was not just a body, but a mental and psychic being capable of living, acting, and traveling independent of her physical organism. You will have bodies to infinity. Actually, you will never be without a body, as you are on an endless journey which knows no end.

Extrasensory Perception and the Man from Calcutta Who Saved His Daughter's Life

In Honolulu, where I am writing this chapter, I had a most interesting conversation with an old friend whom I had known previously in India. I shall call him Harry. He has been practicing traveling clairvoyance, or astral excursions, for many years. His daughter is studying in Honolulu and had been very ill, actually at the point of death. A cable was sent to him in Calcutta, and the moment he received it, he adopted a Yoga posture, closing his eyes, and got into a passive, quiet, receptive state of mind. He visualized his fourth-dimensional, or astral body emerging through his head with all his faculties, and he decreed firmly, knowingly, and with deep conviction: "I want to appear instantly to my daughter and minister to her." He repeated this command about six times, then dropped off into a profound slumber.

Immediately he found himself at his daughter's bedside. She was asleep but awakened immediately and exclaimed to him: "Dad, why didn't you tell me you were coming? Help me." He placed his hands upon her and chanted certain religious phrases and told her, "You will arise in a few hours and be well."

She had an instantaneous healing. Her fever immediately subsided and she shouted to the nurse, "I am healed! I am well! My father was here and he healed me!" The nurse thought she was raving, but the resident physician confirmed the silent, inner knowing of her soul that she was, indeed, perfectly well. However, both laughed at her story of a visitation by her father from India.

The Nurse Heard Nobody in the Room

The nurse was puzzled and perplexed, and said to the daughter: "How could your father or anybody else get in from downstairs through closed doors? I saw no one enter your room."

The daughter explained to the nurse, "Oh, my father visited me in his astral body and laid his hands on me and prayed with me."

The nurse said, "I don't believe in ghosts, apparitions or voodoo." The girl realized that further explanations would be useless.

Harry said that he was perfectly conscious all the time. Considering the distance between Calcutta and Honolulu and the time difference, he discovered that he had been absent from his physical body just ten minutes in all.

Harry is a medical doctor and has tremendous faith in spiritual healing and is very familiar with the many schools of healing. He realized his presence gave a tremendous transfusion of faith, confidence, and courage to his daughter, which impregnated her subconscious mind, and according to his belief and that of his daughter, it was done unto her.

The Bible says, *If thou canst believe, all things are possible to him that believeth* (Mark 9:23).

POINTS TO REMEMBER

1. When involved in a court case, know that Infinite Intelligence guides and directs your attorney, the

judge and all concerned in the case. Realize that the Divine law of harmony prevails, and that you will experience justice and right action in the decision.

2. A salesman, who is suffering from abnormal jealousy and who annoys his wife by checking up on her five or six times a day on long distance telephone calls, heals himself by frequent silent periods during the day when he is away from home. Making a habit of this mental picture, he succeeded in obliterating the jealous pattern in his subconscious based on his sense of insecurity and fear.

3. Nightmares are usually due to a sense of guilt wherein you feel you should be punished. They are based upon the fires of resentment, hostility, or suppressed rage. Your subconscious mind is amenable to control by your conscious mind; therefore, all you have to do is to forgive yourself as well as others and feed your subconscious mind prior to sleep with life-giving patterns of love and harmony, and you will sleep in peace and wake in joy.

4. Everyone dreams. Your dreams are a dramatization of your subconscious mind's contents—a sort of mental television program. Your dreams also aid you in releasing excess tensions and anxieties. Every night, on retiring, fill your conscious mind with the truths of God and you will crowd out of your subconscious everything unlike God.

5. When you are having trouble with an associate who is difficult and hostile, the first thing to do is to quiet your mind periodically and affirm boldly: "The free-flowing love of God saturates my whole being. The Spirit in me salutes the Spirit in _____ and there are love, peace, and understanding between us." Whenever you meet or speak to the other, silently affirm, "I surround you with a circle of love and light."

6. A girl who found herself out of her body frequently commanded her subconscious prior to sleep to find her father, who deserted her mother when the daughter was two years old. Her subconscious obeyed her command of conviction, and she found herself projected as an astral body into a hotel room in Australia. There she spoke to her father and asked him to return, telling him who she was. He looked upon her visit as an apparition, but subsequently realized that it was really his daughter. He eventually returned to a joyous reunion with his wife and daughter.

7. You possess a subtle body now. Some call it the astral body, which is an exact duplicate of your present body, but it operates at a much higher frequency and can enter closed doors and collapse time and space. It is the same as your present body—the only difference is that your astral body oscillates at a higher psychic frequency.

8. Many people become adept at traveling outside their bodies. They possess all their faculties and are able to see, hear, feel, and converse with others as well as describe what they see. They can even move ponderable objects. They can change their directions by commands to their subconscious mind, which obeys.

9. A father living in India, on hearing of his daughter's dangerous illness, quiets his mind and issues a psychic command to his subconscious to project him to his daughter's bedside in Honolulu. He places his hands upon her and prays, and she has a remarkable recovery. He is tangible and real and able to enter the hospital and her room even through closed doors.

13

How to Increase Your Wealth with Psychic Perception

To become aware of the law of plenty, all you have to do is to observe the prodigality or generosity of nature. You will be forced to come to the conclusion that nature is lavish, extravagant, and bountiful. Notice how, for example, when you put seeds into the ground, they come forth ten-fold, a hundred-fold and a thousand-fold. When you gaze at an acorn you are looking at a potential forest.

How a Businessman Realized There Was Unlimited Wealth for Him

Recently, when I was talking with a businessman in Hilo, which is on the west coast of the big island of Hawaii, he told me about a most interesting experience he had had which helped him overcome his poverty complex. One day when he was thinking about how he could pay the bills which had accumulated in his store, he noticed the rain coming down in torrents, and he said to himself: "God's riches are flowing to me like the rain falls from the heavens." He kept this picture in his mind for about a half an hour. Suddenly he had a strange feeling that the atmosphere all around him was filled with God's riches—spiritual, mental, and material—and a marvelous sense of peace came to him.

From that day on, people in steadily increasing numbers came into his store and his sales increased to such a proportion that he had to hire two extra salesladies. What actually happened was that as he meditated on and pictured God's wealth flowing to him like rain, he conveyed this idea to his subconscious mind, which responded accordingly and brought it to pass in a wonderful way. He said to me that he has never worried about money since that day, as it is circulating freely in his experience. He has a card affixed to his desk, which says: *I will rain bread from heaven for you* (Exodus 16:4).

Your Invisible Means of Support

A young millionnaire who frequently comes to my lectures said to me the other day that the trouble with most of the men associated with him is that they have no invisible means of support and that they have no idea of how to tap the treasure house of their subconscious, where infinite riches* are; therefore, the law of plenty cannot operate in their lives. There is an inexhaustible reservoir within you in which everything has its origin and source. You can tap it and grow rich.

She Based Her Success on Service

A young woman who is extraordinarily successful in the beauty parlor business told me that she opened her shop on what she called a shoestring, but her main idea was to give the best service possible to her clients while at the same time

---

*Dr. Joseph Murphy, *Your Infinite Power to be Rich,* (West Nyack, N.Y.: Parker Publishing Company, Inc., 1966).

possessing a sense of unity with the Divine Source in her inner life. She realized that hard work in her business was not enough—that she would have to work also in the inner recesses of her mind.

Her constant prayer formula was the reiteration and understanding of the following great truths: *Thou wilt keep him in perfect peace, whose mind is stayed on thee* (Isaiah 26:3). *In quietness and in confidence shall be your strength* (Isaiah 30:15). *Rest in the Lord, and wait patiently for him* (Psalm 37:7). *Commit thy way unto the Lord; trust also in him; and he shall bring it to pass* (Psalm 37:5).

As she mentally focused on these eternal verities, she knew they would be integrated into her character and mentality and also be expressed in her work. She has been carried forward on the crest of the wave of prosperity, victory, and achievement.

The Law of Being Is Abundance

As you look around you, it is apparent that the infinite treasure house within you creates profusion in all nature. The law of life is plenty—not lack. It is necessary for you to get on a mental and spiritual basis, and then you will be able to transform your life and thus experience the riches of the infinite in your mind, body and business life.

Remember, your thought takes form in the inner realm of your mind and may be seen by a sensitive or psychic person. Poverty thoughts will cause you to experience poverty and stricken conditions. You will find people, perhaps living on the same block or working beside you in an office or factory, who are thinking thoughts of riches, plenty, security, and the life more abundant. They seem to become surrounded with everything they need. The secret of their success is to substitute for the thoughts of lack and limitation the habitual thoughts of the infinite and inexhaustible supply of God's riches. Change your thoughts and *keep them changed.* As you steer and direct your thoughts on the riches of the infinite flowing into your experience, a fantastic and tremendous difference will take place in your life.

How He Overcame His Arrearage in Rent and Overdrawn Bank Account

Some months ago, I gave a lecture in Laguna Beach, California, on the law of opulence. After the lecture a man came to see me at the hotel. He was deeply perturbed. His problem was that he had to mortgage his life policy and could not pay his bills. The rent was three months past due and his purse was empty. His question was: How can I trust in the Infinite Source when I am now broke?"

I replied that there is an answer to every question and that there is a solution to every problem, and the answer to his problem was to follow the Biblical injunction: *Seek ye first the Kingdom of God, and His righteousness; and all these things shall be added unto you* (Matthew 6:33). This means that all the powers of the God-presence are within you. You must claim what you want and feel the reality of it, and your subconscious mind will honor, validate and manifest that which you impress upon it.

I explained to him that wealth, health, peace of mind, success, etc. were all simply states of mind and that one idea, such as a new invention, a book, a play, a new technique in business, or a promotional concept to benefit and bless mankind, could be worth a million dollars or more. Righteousness simply means the right use of the law, such as right thinking, right feeling, and right action. You wish for all men all the blessings of life. You perceive abundance in all things for all people.

He began to see that a change of view could solve his problem and redeem him. I gave him a very simple way to disperse his dark and depressing mood by pointing out to him the tremendous power of words in activating the latent powers within him. The following words were to be affirmed out loud for one-half hour three times a day: "Wealth success, victory, joy." He put all the feeling and enthusiasm at his command into these words, and gradually he became lifted up; he found that these words, sincerely uttered, activated and made alive the real powers and potencies of his subconscious mind.

As he anchored his mind on these realities and principles, the conditions and circumstances corresponding to their nature became visible on the screen of space. A few weeks went by and nothing particular happened other than that some close friends advanced him a few thousand dollars to tide him over; however, the solution came about a month later, when he discovered that one of his friends who had helped him out financially, as mentioned above, had also given him a ticket on the Irish Sweepstakes. To his amazement, his horse won, and he received a large sum of money which solved all his financial problems. His subconscious knew the answer. He trusted the inner powers, and according to his belief it was done unto him.

A Fruitful Technique for Wealth and Success

Many people say, "If I affirm, 'I am successful' when I am a failure, or if I say to myself, 'I am wealthy' when I am broke, I am lying to myself, and I seem to get worse and experience the opposite of what I affirm or claim to be true."

The reason for this is that the belief in lack, failure, and limitation is dominant in their subconscious mind, and every time they affirm wealth, they resurrect the thought of lack. They fail to understand how to tap the riches of the Infinite, because they don't know the workings of their mind.

For those who honestly feel that lack of understanding, I recommend a very simple procedure by asking them a simple question: Do you believe in wealth, that bountiful wealth exists, and that the Infinite cannot fail? It is all-powerful and there is nothing to oppose it. Therefore, success is a principle of life. For example, walk down the street or go out into the country. All you see is wealth, created either by man or by God. All created things were ideas, either in the mind of man or of God. I suggest, therefore, two words, which are not mere abstractions, but words (thoughts expressed) which have tremendous power, as they relate to the inexhaustible power and wisdom of the Infinite. By repeating the two words slowly, quietly, feelingly, and knowingly—"success, wealth"—and doing this over and over again many times a day, you get your ego out of the way, and there is no contradiction in your conscious or subconscious mind, as you agree there are such things as wealth and success.

When you use certain constructive words—words which stand for and represent eternal truths of God—then your mind becomes anchored on the only Presence, Cause, Power, and Substance, and results follow. Use these words regularly, systematically, and repetitiously, and you will discover you are on a sound, scientific path. Remember, it is your attitude of mind that is to be overcome, not your circumstances. When you possess the right mental attitude, your conditions, experiences, and financial status will automatically right themselves.

A Businessman Discovered Why Wealth Flowed from Him Instead of to Him

A businessman complained to me that he worked very hard, and spent long hours in his store, yet one block away another man in exactly the same business and with a much smaller store deposited in the bank three times as much as he did every week. He was constantly comparing his meager results with those of another and had become envious and also somewhat resentful.

I explained to him that by entertaining envious thoughts he was actually impoverishing himself, and that this was one of the worst possible attitudes to hold, because his negative thinking and his feeling of inferiority were definitely blocking his expansion and growth along all lines. So long as he retained this mental posture, wealth would flow from him instead of to him.

The remedy was very simple. All he had to do was to bless and sincerely wish greater prosperity and success for his so-called competitor whose apparently more successful and prosperous state had incited him to envy. Accordingly, he prayed as follows: "I recognize God as my instant and everlasting supply. God's wealth flows to me in avalanches of abundance, and I am Divinely directed to give better service every day. I know, believe, and rejoice that God is prospering the businessman in the next block, and I sincerely wish for him all the blessings of life."

When any thought of envy toward the other businessman came to his mind, he would affirm: "God is prospering you." After a while the envious thoughts lost all momentum, and he too began to prosper—and beyond his fondest dreams at that. This man found that the cause of his financial lack and straitened circumstances had been due to his state of mind. By blessing those whose prosperity and success annoy us or excite our envy or jealousy, and by wishing that they become even more affluent and successful in every way, we heal our own minds and open the door to the riches of the Infinite.

Out of the abundance of your heart, you can pour out the gifts of love, light, joy, success, and goodwill to all; and you will discover that by blessing others, you too are blessed, and all sense of envy, inferiority, and poverty is overcome.

The Magic Key to Wealth and Promotion in Life

In consultation periods over many years, I have discovered that the reason many men and women do not get promoted and make more money in their profession or business is that they were in the habit of condemning those who went up the ladder of life, while stating that others in their organization were cold, callous, ruthless, and that some even had a "racket." They failed to perceive that there is nothing more destructive and more calculated to deprive them of promotion and advancement than condemning and judging harshly those who succeeded, and who received increments and advancement in their work. Actually, I found out that they let wealth, honor, and riches slip through their fingers and blocked and impeded their own progress spiritually, mentally, and financially.

The remedy in all cases was to teach them to wish sincerely for all those around them as well as all people everywhere that they be blessed and prospered in countless ways, and by rejoicing in their advancement and material progress. The result inevitably is that they are delivered from the mental block of envy, covetousness, and resentment. They then become dispensers of God's bounty to all. By praying in the above manner, unhappy people came back to their Divine center and they discovered that the Infinite Being was pouring out blessing and benedictions upon themselves and for all those for whom they prayed. By wishing others well, you are blessing yourself. Remember the old Hindu maxim: "The ship that comes home to my brother comes home to me."

POINTS TO REMEMBER

1. To become aware of the law of plenty, all you have to do is to observe the prodigality of nature. Nature is lavish, extravagant, and bountiful. Contemplate the abundance of nature and you will experience the life more abundant.

2. A technique to attract riches into your life is to affirm frequently: "God's riches are flowing to me like the rain falls from the heavens." Repeat it

frequently and you will succeed in impregnating your subconscious mind with the idea of riches.

3. The trouble with most people who don't have all the money they need to accomplish their life objectives is that they lack the invisible psychic means of support. They fail to see that the treasure house of eternity is within them.

4. A beauty parlor operator discovered that the key to her outstanding success was her intense desire to give greater and better service to her clients. She did her very best externally, but she also worked internally by turning to the Infinite within her, claiming peace, harmony, power and guidance. She realized that the inside governs the outside. The inner world of the mind and the outer objective activity must work together in unison and in concord.

5. The law of life is plenty, not lack. Your thoughts have form, shape, and substance in your mind. When nourished and sustained by faith, they come forth as form and expression on the screen of space. Your thoughts of opulence, harmony, security, and the riches of the Infinite will manifest in your life provided you change your thoughts and keep them changed.

6. There is a way out of every problem and an answer to every question. Whatever you seek in life, you must go within the psychic recesses of your mind and there claim that you now are what you long to be, that you now possess what you long to possess, and your subconscious mind will reproduce what you claim and feel to be true. The Kingdom of God is the kingdom of Infinite Intelligence and Infinite Power within you. The riches of the Infinite are within you, and you must claim your inheritance

which was given to you from the foundation of time.

7. Repeating frequently the words "wealth, success, victory, joy" will activate these powers and qualities within you, and your subconscious will release all these potentialities within you, and wonders will happen in your life. The ways of your subconscious are past finding out, and the money you seek may come from a bequest, a sweepstake ticket, or an idea may well up from your subconscious worth a fortune.

8. To obviate a quarrel in your mind, instead of saying, "I am wealthy, I am successful, I am happy," etc., use the words (thoughts expressed) "wealth, success, happiness." These words, which are thoughts expressed, have their own mechanics and mathematics within them, and by repetition activate these dormant powers in your subconscious, and you will be compelled to express these characteristics and qualities, as the law of your subconscious is compulsion.

9. Envy, covetousness, and resentment impoverish you, as these are thoughts of lack and limitation and are very negative. You are the thinker in your universe; therefore, you attract more lack, limitation, and misery. Radiate thoughts of love, peace, prosperity and success to all those around you, knowing what you wish for others you are wishing for yourself. Love is the fulfilling of the law of success, prosperity and abundance. Love is goodwill to all.

10. Recognize God as your instant and everlasting supply, and claim that God's wealth is forever circulating in your life, and wealth will flow to you in avalanches of abundance.

11. Criticism, condemnation, and jealousy of others because they have gone up the ladder of success and fame will block your good and inhibit the flow of God's riches to you. Pour out the benediction and the blessing of the Infinite on all those who excite your envy, and you will open the door for countless blessings for yourself.

14

How Your Perception
Brings You Wonders
of Disciplined Imagination

The following are perceptive statements on the subject of imagination made by many great thinkers:

> We are all of us imaginative in some form or other, for images are the brood of desire.
>
> George Eliot

> Imagination rules the world.
>
> Napoleon

> The soul without imagination is what an observatory would be without a telescope.
>
> H. W. Beecher

> Thought convinces; feeling persuades. If imagination furnishes the fact with wings, feeling is the great, stout muscle which flies them, and lifts them from the ground. Thought sees beauty; emotion feels it.
>
> Theodore Parker

Imagination, the image-making power, common to all who have the gift of dreams.

I. R. Lowell

Imagination disposes of everything; it creates beauty, justice, and happiness, which are everything in the world.

Pascal

Imagination is the eye of the soul.

Joubert

The poet's eye, in a fine frenzy rolling, doth glance from heaven to earth, from earth to heaven; and as imagination bodies forth the forms of things unknown, the poet's pen turns them to shape, and gives to airy nothing a local habitation and a name.

Shakespeare

Imagination is more powerful than knowledge.

Albert Einstein

The dictionary defines imagination as the action of forming mental images or concepts of what is not actually present to the senses. It is your ability to meet and resolve difficulties; resourcefulness; to solve business problems with imagination; a job that requires imagination.

Imagination is one of the primal faculties of your mind and, like any other power, you can use it constructively or destructively and reap results according to the way you use your mental images. In this chapter, the author refers to disciplined, controlled and divinely directed imagination. When you use your imaginative power wisely and harmoniously, you can project and clothe your ideas, plans, and purposes, giving them visibility on the screen of space.

How She Made the Impossible Possible

Some months ago I had a long telephone conversation with a woman in Georgia, whom we shall call Mrs. X. She said that because of the high interest rates and the high price for her home, the real estate agents had not been able to get a single client even to look at it. Her husband had passed on and she was living alone in the house, while at the same time suffering from financial stress and strain due to her inability to keep up the payments and taxes.

I gave her the following simple technique: Sit still, relax, immobilize your attention, and focus your mind's eye on the check for $100,000 which is what you want for the house. Touch the check with your imaginary hands, feel and perceive its reality, give thanks for it, and repeat this "mental movie" for four or five minutes several times a day; gradually you will find the image will sink into your subconscious mind. When you succeed in conveying the mental image to your subconscious, the latter will bring it to pass.

A few weeks went by, and Mrs. X wrote, saying that she had sold the house to a research professor who had come from New York with his four children. He saw that it was the ideal home for him. She said that she had become very still and sleepy and had imagined the check for $100,000 made out in her name, and in her imagination she had gone into the local bank and deposited it. All this had taken place in her mental imagery. She had done this for four or five minutes at intervals of one hour each day for two weeks. After that she had had no further desire to dramatize the event in her mind, as a feeling of peace and relaxation had come over her and she knew intuitively that her prayer was answered. This professor saw the sign "For sale by owner," and the minute he walked in the door, he said, "This is it."

Remember that your imagination, when disciplined, spiritualized, controlled, and directed, becomes the most exalted and noblest attribute of man.

How a Widow of 72 Banished Loneliness

During an interview with Mrs. M, I listened while she gave me all the reasons why she could not get married, instead of all the reasons why she could. Mrs. M complained that although she had written for prayers to all the New Thought Churches to pray for the right husband for her, all the effort had come to naught. She said that her children were grown up, married, and living as far as 3,000 miles away, and that while she had met many widowers in her retirement city, no one had proposed to her.

At my suggestion, Mrs. M practiced an imaginary scene wherein she pictured and felt herself to be in my study where I was conducting the marriage ceremony. She heard my voice saying, "I now pronounce you man and wife." In this imaginary drama, she felt the imaginary ring on her finger. She dramatized this picture in her mind over and over again until she felt it to be so real that when she opened her eyes, she had the feeling that she wasn't in her own home but actually in my study. What had happened was that she had made the whole mental imagery so actual and vivid that she embodied it subconsciously and had no further desire to repeat the mental drama. She developed a high sense of perception.

Shortly afterward, on a trip to visit her son in New York City, Mrs. M met a wonderful retired physician on the train. While she was in New York, he invited her out a few times and shortly thereafter proposed marriage, which she accepted. She had used her imagination wisely by perceiving the end, the finished thing; then her subconscious had brought it to pass in its own way.

By hearing the words "I now pronounce you man and wife" and by feeling the imaginary ring on her finger, she had implied to her subconscious that she was already married mentally to the ideal man who harmonized with her in every way. When you pray, contemplate the happy ending, rejoice in it, and you will experience the joy of the answered prayer.

How Her Perception Established the Mental Equivalent of a Million Dollars

I had the most amazing telephone call from the husband of a woman whom we shall call Mrs. H, saying: "My wife just inherited a million dollars. You told her what to do." Naturally, I congratulated him and wished for both of them all the blessings of life. I recalled talking to her one Sunday after a lecture at the Wilshire Ebell Theatre in Los Angeles at which time she had said that she wanted a million dollars for a certain project which was very sound and constructive. I explained to her that she first had to establish the mental equivalent of a million dollars in her mind, and that she could do this by getting intensely interested in the finished project, looking at it in her mind, rejoicing in the accomplished fact, and giving thanks for the wonder of it all.

She pictured the end in her mind, made it very vivid and real, and every night prior to sleep, she would affirm "a million, a million, a million," over and over again as a lullaby until she fell asleep, knowing her subconscious must sooner or later accept it. At the end of about a month, she was advised by an attorney that she had inherited over a million dollars. It was, as her husband said, "completely out of the blue." Mrs. H had done what Shakespeare said. She gave to ". . . airy nothing a local habitation and a name." Through frequent habitation in her mind, she succeeded in making it a reality, and her subconscious brought it to pass in ways she knew not of.

How to Become Acquainted with the Perceptive Designer Within You

Within you are a designer, an architect, and a weaver. They take the image of your mind and mold it into a pattern of life which brings you peace, joy, and victory. The greatest and richest galleries are the galleries of the mind devoted to wisdom, truth, and beauty.

Picture your ideal in life; live mentally with this ideal. Let the ideal captivate your perceptive imagination. You will move in the direction of the mental image which governs your mind. The ideals of life are like the dew of heaven which move over the arid areas of your mind, refreshing and invigorating you. With your disciplined imagination, you can soar above all appearances, discord, and sense evidence, and imagine the way things ought to be while realizing the sublime principle of harmony operating through, in, and behind all things. Reject the evidence of your senses and realize that the inside controls the outside. Your mental image is the reality, or the inside, and its external manifestation, or form, is the outside.

Why He Called Perceptive Imagination the Workshop of God

Recently I had lunch with an extraordinary young man whom we shall call J. J. He is in the radio and communication field. He has been reading *Your Infinite Power to Be Rich** and he said, "I could quote it by heart." His avocation on weekends is to take his wife to Caliente Race Track. He had been in the habit of losing $10 to $15 weekly at the track, and his wife had said to him that he should use his subconscious mind and win a large sum so they could buy a new home in Beverly Hills.

Accordingly, he began to still his mind every night for about 15 minutes and in a quiet, passive way, he would imagine the cashier giving him a check for $50,000 and saying to him, "Boy, you're lucky." He felt himself at the cashier's window and he imagined hearing the voice of the

---

*Dr. Joseph Murphy, *Your Infinite Power to Be Rich* (West Nyack, N.Y.: Parker Publishing Company, Inc., 1966).

cashier. He looked at the check, touched it with his imaginary hands, and rejoiced and gave thanks for it. In his vivid, intense, dramatic, and imaginative way, he showed the check to his wife, saying: "Honey, the house you wanted is yours." In this imaginary drama, she would exclaim, "It is wonderful!" over and over again.

He rehearsed this drama in his mind night after night for about a month. He said that sometimes this scenic drama was so real, vivid, and seemingly tangible that when he opened his eyes he was amazed to find himself in his bedroom instead of at the race track. This state of mind is indicative of success in conveying the picture to the subconscious mind.

The fifth week after beginning the above-mentioned technique, he went to Caliente and was, as he said, absolutely confident that he would get the check he had pictured and felt as true subjectively. He bet rather large sums on six races and they were all winners. As he presented his tickets to the cashier, the cashier gave him a check for $50,000, saying to him exactly as he had subjectively affirmed every night for over a month, "Boy, you're lucky."

He is now living in a lovely home in Beverly Hills, for which he paid the $50,000 received at Caliente. Because of a vast increase in value of real estate in the last few years, it is now worth double that price. He and his wife have never been to the races since that day several years ago, as they are both too busy working every day in the radio and television field helping to heal the wounds of man.

Sir Winston Churchill once said, "This is an age in which the mental attitude decides the fortunes of people rather than the fortunes decide the mood." The ancient Hebrews said, "Imagination is the workshop of God." Psychic perception is your key to constructive imagination.

POINTS TO REMEMBER

1. Your psychic imagination is your capacity to form

mental images or concepts of what is not actually present to the physical senses.

2. Imagination is one of the foremost faculties of your mind. When disciplined, it enables you to clothe your ideas, dreams, or aspirations and project them on the screen of space.

3. Regardless of evidence of senses, you can imagine that you have sold your home. Feel the reality of the sale mentally, looking at the imaginary check in your imaginary hands, feeling it, rejoicing in it, and repeating the drama over and over again until you sense the subjective reality of it. You will know when you have succeeded in conveying the mental picture to your mind, the reason being that a sense of peace and inner knowing arises, whereby you know that you know. It is an intuitive awareness.

4. A simple technique in attracting the right marriage partner was employed by a 72-year-old widow. All she did was to imagine that I was in front of her in my study, and in her imagination she heard me say over and over again, "I now pronounce you man and wife." She felt the imaginary ring on her finger, which implied to her that she was already married. The whole mental movie, which she dramatized repeatedly, intensively, and joyously, conveyed to her that she was already married to the ideal man who harmonized with her in every way. After a few weeks she actually met the man of her dream, and they were married. The law is that whatever you imagine and feel to be true sinks into your subconscious mind, which in turn brings it to pass.

5. A woman wanted a million dollars for a wonderful project for herself and her husband. She realized she had to establish the mental psychic equivalent before she could receive it. Accordingly, every night she would imagine she was looking at the finished pro-

ject and giving thanks for the wonders of it all; at the same time, she would silently, feelingly, and knowingly lull herself to sleep every night with the one word "million," knowing that her subconscious mind was aware it was a million dollars she needed. At the end of a month, her husband called me, saying: "My wife just inherited a million dollars out of the blue." She had succeeded in establishing the mental or psychic equivalent in her subconscious mind by reiterating "a million" over and over again and by picturing the completed million-dollar project. She knew that ideas are conveyed to the subconscious by repetition.

6. Picture your ideal in life; live mentally with this ideal, and you will move in the direction of the ideal which governs your mind.

7. A young radio engineer wanted to buy a home for his wife and didn't have the money. His avocation was the study of the racing sheet and betting $10 or $15 weekly but with negative results. He read *Your Infinite Power to Be Rich,** one of my popular books, and he began to use his imagination wisely, constructively, and judiciously. He imagined himself at the cashier's window at Caliente Race Track receiving a check for $50,000 and felt the solidity and tangibility of the cashier's cage. In his vivid imaginary scene, the cashier said to him, "Boy, you're lucky." In about a month's time he succeeded in impregnating his subconscious mind, and on subsequently visiting the race track, he literally won $50,000.

---

*Dr. Joseph Murphy, *Your Infinite Power to Be Rich* (West Nyack, N.Y.: Parker Publishing Company, Inc., 1966).

15

How to Know
the Mysterious Perceptive Powers
of Your Mind

You have a conscious and a subconscious* mind. These represent two phases or functions of your mind. Sometimes they are referred to as the objective and subjective mind. With your conscious mind you reason, analyze, and make use of your five senses to govern your contact with the world. Your conscious mind reasons inductively and deductively. Your subconscious mind is the seat of memory, emotions and intuition. It is the seat of clairvoyance, clairaudience, telekinesis, and telepathy.

In your subconscious you will find infinite intelligence and boundless wisdom and all the riches of the Infinite waiting for you to tap. In a passive, psychic state it is possible for a good sensitive to read your thoughts, even to the minutest detail; he (or she) may even read a sealed letter in

---

*See *The Power of Your Subconscious Mind* by Dr. Joseph Murphy, Prentice-Hall, Inc., Englewood Cliffs, New Jersey, 1963.

your pocket which you have not yet read yourself. Many have developed the clairvoyant powers of their subconscious to the extent that they have the ability to see events happening at a distance and independent of their five senses.

Your subconscious is sometimes referred to as the soul. A very important thing to remember is that your subconscious mind is constantly amenable to suggestion. For example, if you are placed in a hypnotic state, your subconscious mind will accept without hesitation every suggestion made by the operator, no matter how absurd or incongruous it may seem to your conscious mind.

What Experiences Reveal about Your Subconscious

For example, the author has witnessed many hypnotic experiments in different parts of the world. In one, he has seen a man put into a trance and told by the psychologist that he was a dog. The man accepted the suggestion and played the role of a dog to the best of his ability, lapping up milk from a plate, barking, etc. In other experiments, when a man is told that he is President Roosevelt, and if he is old enough to remember the former president's voice, mannerisms, and gestures, he will reenact the role with the vocal intonations characteristic of Mr. Roosevelt.

Remember, your subconscious is amenable to the power of suggestion and acts upon it, whether the suggestion given is true or false. Your subconscious brings it to a logical conclusion based on the premise given it while your conscious mind is suspended and in abeyance. Your subconscious does not reason like your conscious mind but accepts the idea given it; and, working by deduction, it responds according to the nature of the suggestion given. It is absolutely essential that you understand this mode of operation; otherwise, you may be tricked, deceived, and fooled by all manner of fraudulent operators. You must intuitively perceive all this deception.

He Was Told He Was Possessed by a Devil

Some years ago in London, England, I witnessed a medical doctor hypnotize a seminary student called Pat. He suggested to Pat that he was possessed by devils. Immediately the student turned pale, shook with terror, and began to scream and yell. He was about to go into convulsions, but the doctor immediately removed the suggestion and told him he was free now, calm, peaceful and perfectly well. When he awakened he had no memory of what had happened and was completely relaxed and at ease.

It is easy to understand what happened. First of all, of course, there is no such thing as a devil or the condition of being possessed by devils, but Pat believed in a devil and devils; therefore, he saw what he believed to be devils—half man and half beast with cloven hooves, horns of a goat, and a fiery tail which stings. These forms were what we call subjective hallucinations based on portrayals of devils given to Pat when he was a boy. The actual devils which haunt us, when we lose our perceptive faculties, are fear, ignorance, superstition, hate, jealousy, remorse, etc.

How Pat Described Heaven

Pat was again hypnotized and told he was in heaven. He was asked to describe what he saw. Immediately his countenance changed; he seemed peaceful, joyous, and almost ecstatic. He told us all about the beautiful angels who were there, and he saw a magnificent golden throne, and sitting on the throne a man who seemed to be a great sage. The man, who looked like Jesus, had a scripture in his hand. Pat also heard beautiful music, which he described as a celestial choir.

It is obvious to anyone who is informed on this subject that since the subconscious mind is controlled by suggestion, the imaginary picture Pat saw of heaven was based on his early boyhood beliefs and theological instructions. He believed that heaven was a place where you go when you die.

The suggestion of the doctor simply activated his subconscious beliefs and opinions and dramatized his premise, though false, to what seemed to be a logical conclusion.

Remember this clearly: The suggestions given to Pat in the trance state, whether true or false, were reasoned deductively only and dramatized by his subconscious with marvelous acumen and sagacity.

Experiments on Medical Students and How Many Drank Water and Became Drunk

Another interesting experiment conducted by this same medical man was that of hypnotizing two medical students who were present. To one he gave soap shavings and told him it was a banana and that he would relish it, digest it, and feel good afterwards. This student ate the soap shavings and had no subsequent gastric distress. To another hypnotized student, he said he had a very high temperature and rapid pulse and was perspiring copiously. All these symptoms were manifested immediately.

Mary, in the trance state, was given a glass of water and told it was Irish whiskey. She became highly intoxicated, murmuring gibberish and staggering all over the place. The doctor gave her a tablespoonful of water and told her that it was a specific drug from Germany which would instantly bring about sobriety and peace of mind. His mere suggestion acted as the perfect antidote for Mary. When she was awakened she felt absolutely normal and at peace.

This demonstrates the amenability of the subconscious to suggestion as well as its creative power.

Your Auto-Suggestion Can Prevent You from Being Hypnotized

You cannot be hypnotized by another provided you convey to your subconscious the idea that no one can hypnotize you without your consent. Hypnosis is usually induced by the suggestion of the operator. His failure to hypnotize you is due to your suggestion to your subconscious that he cannot do it. Your auto-suggestion is more powerful than his suggestion; this is why he fails. All this is due to the way your subconscious works; the stronger suggestion always prevails.

The Reason Why the Hypnotist Failed

Some years ago I attended a series of experiments on hypnosis in the home of an outstanding lawyer-psychologist in New York City. He hypnotized a young girl and repeatedly suggested to her that she should disrobe. This was in the presence of about 12 men and women. She refused to cooperate in any way, and seemed highly disturbed and distressed. The psychologist seemed confounded by her stubborn resistance because he had boasted she would do anything he told her to do when she was in the hypnotic state. He had expected passive obedience, which he did not get because he was unaware of the subtle role of the counter-suggestion this girl had given to herself. She retained her perception.

Your subconscious always accepts the more dominant of two ideas or suggestions. The girl's auto-suggestion, prior to the hypnotic sleep experiment, was this: "I will do absolutely nothing contrary to my moral or religious code. My subconscious accepts this."

This demonstrates that suggestion is the controlling power governing your subconscious. Your subconscious is amenable to the suggestions of your own conscious mind just as well as that of another. In the waking state you can always reject the suggestions of others and think on whatsoever things are true, lovely, and of good report.

How She Was Freed from a So-Called Evil Spirit

From the foregoing illustration, you can see how your subconscious mind operates. Last year, while I was on a speaking engagement in San Francisco, a woman came to see me at the hotel complaining that a discarnate entity who was an evil spirit was constantly annoying her by pouring out vulgarisms, obscenities and maledictions, commanding her to violate her sex code, and even scratching her at night. Recently he had been telling her to jump into the ocean and commit suicide.

She had been taking tranquilizers and had had some psychiatric consultations, but nothing seemed to do her any good. This woman seemed frightened out of her wits. She told me that many times, night and day, this so-called entity kept saying to her: "Take an overdose of Seconal. Go ahead. Go ahead, kill yourself."

The Cause of Her Inner Turmoil

This woman, who believed in the literal interpretation of the Bible and in evil spirits possessing her soul, did not understand that the devils mentioned in the Bible were simply personifications of hate, resentment, remorse, self-condemnation, anger, and hostility, as well as other destructive emotions which are generated by destructive, negative thoughts enthroned in the mind.

She had been practicing automatic writing for some months. This means that she held a pencil in her hand, believing some invisible spirit would guide her hand. According to the law of suggestion, her own subconscious mind accepted the suggestion given it, and gradually it assumed control of the muscles and nerves of her hand and propelled her pencil. Her conscious mind was passive and quiescent, and as she pointed out, objectively speaking, she was oblivious to what she was writing down. She was also fearful that evil powers might write through her.

Moreover, she felt guilty and had a deep resentment towards her husband, for he was impotent and completely depleted sexually. The voices she heard which cursed God, her Bible, and herself were merely a playback from the poisonous food she had been feeding her subconscious mind.

She Didn't Know the Power of Auto-Suggestion

The entity that she believed to be speaking to her was in actual fact her own suggestion of fear. Job said: *That which I greatly feared is come upon me* (Job 3:25). This woman associated her automatic writing with the idea of spirits, not knowing that it was actually her subconscious mind reproducing what she had impressed upon it. Her subconscious was dominated by fear, guilt (because she hated her husband), plus the fact that she believed she should and would be punished because of her deep-seated resentment and hostility. These voices seemed like another personality, when actually they were a dramatization of the negative contents of her subconscious. Actually, she was talking to herself.

How She Healed Herself and Experienced Peace of Mind

Frankly, I think my explanation to her was 90 percent of the healing process. I explained to her that it is absolutely impossible for negative and destructive voices and emotions to dwell in a mind dedicated and consecrated to the God-Presence within one, and that all she had to do was to fill her mind with the truths of God, which would then crowd out of her mind everything unlike God, or the truth.

Accordingly, at my suggestion, morning, noon, and night, she repeated out loud the words of the great healing and protective 91st Psalm, knowing that as she affirmed these truths, they would neutralize, obliterate, and expunge from her subconscious all the negative patterns lodged in the recesses of her deeper mind. She made the 91st Psalm a vital part of her life, and whenever any negative voice or thought came to her from her deeper self, she would affirm immediately: "God loves me and cares for me."

After about ten days, these destructive voices lost all momentum and she found herself at peace. You can saturate your mind by repeating the marvelous spiritual gems of the 91st Psalm:

> *He that dwelleth in the secret place of the most High shall abide under the shadow of the Almighty.*
>
> *I will say of the Lord, He is my refuge and my fortress: my God; in him will I trust.*
>
> *Surely he shall deliver thee from the snare of the fowler, and from the noisome pestilence.*
>
> *He shall cover thee with his feathers, and under his wings shalt thou trust: his truth shall be thy shield and buckler.*
>
> *Thou shalt not be afraid for the terror by night; nor for the arrow that flieth by day;*
>
> *Nor for the pestilence that walketh in darkness; nor for the destruction that wasteth at noonday.*
>
> *A thousand shall fall at thy side, and ten thousand at thy right hand; but it shall not come nigh thee.*
>
> *Only with thine eyes shalt thou behold and see the reward of the wicked.*
>
> *Because thou hast made the Lord, which is my refuge, even the most High, thy habitation;*
>
> *There shall no evil befall thee, neither shall any plague come nigh thy dwelling.*
>
> *For he shall give his angels charge over thee, to keep thee in all thy ways.*
>
> *They shall bear thee up in their hands, lest thou dash thy foot against a stone.*
>
> *Thou shalt tread upon the lion and adder: the young lion and the dragon shalt thou trample under feet.*

> *Because he hath set his love upon me, there-*
> *fore will I deliver him: I will set him on high,*
> *because he hath known my name.*
>   *He shall call upon me, and I will answer him:*
> *I will be with him in trouble; I will deliver him, and*
> *honour him.*
>   *With long life will I satisfy him, and shew him*
> *my salvation.*

The above will surely increase your sense of psychic perception.

How She Discovered Who Was Operating the Ouija Board

My secretary Mrs. Wright, the mother of two extraordinarily brilliant young men, just informed me that some years ago when she was a teenager, her grandmother and she had spent many happy hours operating the ouija board and receiving wonderful messages from supposedly unseen intelligences. The ouija board was apparently propelled by some unseen power, and the pointer spelled out answers to all questions asked.

Mrs. Wright did not know at that time how the conscious and subconscious mind function, and she did not believe in any supernatural entities or discarnate spirits operating the ouija instrument. The terms "spiritualism" and "spiritualistic phenomena" also meant nothing to her at that time.

One day she asked the ouija board, "Who is writing and who is answering my questions?" The ouija spelled out, "Louise Barrows." Louise is her middle name and Barrows was her name prior to her marriage to her husband, Stan Wright. This experiment demonstrates clearly that at the time that Mrs. Wright operated the ouija board she knew nothing about spiritualistic phenomena; therefore, her subconscious mind did not assume it was a spirit speaking. Had she believed that some deceased relative was responding, naturally, according to the law of suggestion, her subconscious would have played the role of a deceased relative.

Her grandmother, who rejected the hypothesis that invisible entities operated the ouija board and sent answers from the next dimension of life, asked the ouija board, "Is it my own mind answering me?" The answer spelled out was "only you." If she had entertained the idea that it was a deceased person or some disembodied spirit operating, her subconscious would have assumed the role and would have answered accordingly.

Actually, it was the subconscious mind operating the ouija board, and these people were just talking to themselves. The law of parsimony or the simplicity in assumptions in logical formulation must precede all other criteria in arriving at an explanation. The *onus probandi* is placed where it belongs, with those who claim invisible entities for the phenomenon.

A Street-Walker Speaks Like a Goddess

The essence of the following presentation is taken from pages 10 and 11 of *My Personal Recollections of Thomas Troward,* a booklet by Harry Gaze. Permission for publication has been granted by his widow, Dr. Olive Gaze.

The late Dr. Harry Gaze, world lecturer, author, and close friend of the late Judge Thomas Troward, author of *Edinburgh Lectures* and many other books on mental and spiritual laws, revealed an interesting experiment conducted by himself, Dr. Cornwall Round of London, and Judge Thomas Troward. Troward wanted to see Dr. Round perform an experiment with the subconscious mind. Dr. Round was an outstanding physician and surgeon in London and had experimented extensively with hypnosis.

At Dr. Gaze's request, Judge Troward attended the Psycho-Therapeutic Society, and Dr. Round fetched a professional street-walker to whom they paid a very good fee, considerably in excess of her usual honorarium. Dr. Gaze said that she was assured that nothing would happen to hurt her in any way and that she would feel refreshed and stimulated after the hypnotic session.

After hypnotizing her, Dr. Round repeated to her subconscious mind many times, "You are a high priestess in the Temple of the Sun. You have a message for those who are here. You will speak to us clearly and brilliantly. You know great truths. You will tell us about them. You have wise and able associates, and you are open to their wisdom. You are fluent and able. Remember, you are a wise priestess, and you can instruct us."

After much repetition of substantially the same words, her regular, personal characteristics seemed to disappear and a new and more attractive individual appeared. Finally, she lifted herself up proudly and even regally, assumed the impersonation of a goddess, and launched into a discourse in which she talked eloquently and learnedly of life, philosophy, and immortality.

Thomas Troward was profoundly impressed, as were others, some of whom had previously tested hypnosis for medical usage, and sometimes as an anesthetic for minor operations. Judge Troward exclaimed, "This certainly proves that there is a subjective mind that can accept and impersonate what is vividly suggested, when hypnotism has placed the conscious mind in abeyance; but, of course, the thought is the real power." The answer was an elevation of psychic perception.

Interestingly, the company had various views about the source of the phenomenon. One man was positive that the subject matter of the discourse, as well as the changed deportment of the woman, were supplied by a control in the form of a disembodied spirit of great intelligence. He saw in these results a proof of spirit communication. The consensus, however, shared by Judge Troward, Dr. Harry Gaze, and Dr. Round, was that it illustrated the normal powers of the subjective mind, and that the ideas advanced were a composite of the ideas held by those present, or ideas received from the treasury or storehouse of the universal subjective mind.

I have been using information from a written report of an experiment related by the late Dr. Harry Gaze, and the way I look at it is simply that when the subject was in the trance state, she responded to the suggestion of Dr. Round. Her subconscious in turn tapped the contents of the minds of those present, through her psychic perception, who were very familiar with Vedantic philosophy, and Oriental, Buddhist, and Hindu religions.

Her subconscious then, with amazing sagacity and mental acumen, synthesized the various contents resident in the subconscious of all present and presented them in logical sequence, conforming to the nature of the suggestions given by Dr. Round.

Oftentimes You Get a Psychic Message from Yourself

An old friend of mine in New York City experimented with a number of men and women who were self-styled mediums, and who professed to get in touch with relatives in the next dimension. During these experiments he would give his own name and ask for a communication. The medium assumed he had a brother or father in the next dimension, and he always received very comforting and loving messages from an imaginary deceased brother and sometimes even from his father.

In other words, he had a very touching communication from himself, the reason being that the mediums acted on the supposition that his own name represented a deceased relative. The fact is he had no deceased brother or father, which made him even more convinced that it was simply the medium's subconscious reacting to her own suggestions. She had gone into a trance state, suggesting to her subconscious that she would get a communication from the supposed loved one in the next dimension, and her subconscious obliged him with an affectionate message from himself.

There Are Outstanding Exceptions

Not all communications have their origin solely in the subconscious of the sitter or the medium. There are some extraordinary, outstanding mediums of unimpeachable integrity. As you have already deduced from reading this chapter, it is just as easy to receive messages from a living person through an entranced medium as from a so-called dead person, and also from an imaginary person, as from a real one, by making the appropriate suggestion to the subconscious mind.

The late Arthur Ford was one of America's foremost mediums, and there is no doubt that when he was entranced extraordinary and verifiable messages came forth through him. Undoubtedly, in his case, he served as a channel through which communications came from loved ones in the next dimension. Countless listeners testify that they are genuine. For example, I believe that Bishop Pike's communications with his deceased son were authentic and real.

Suppose, for instance, that your father called you from London, England, and suppose someone else was mimicking his voice and pretending to be your father; would you not have all sorts of ways and means of discovering whether it was *really* your father or not? Certain anecdotes, pet names, trivial incidents, and a host of other experiences known only to both of you would soon convince you it was your father.

The late Geraldine Cummins, author of many books investigated by many scientific bodies, was at times undoubtedly in touch with people in the next dimension. It would be foolish to say it is impossible, because we are all mental and spiritual beings, and telepathic contact exists between loved ones all the time.

If you are in Chicago and your mother is in Los Angeles, you can receive a telepathic message from her, and she can also receive one from you. How often have you seen the entire contents of a friend's or relative's letter in your sleep and then received it a few days later and discovered that its contents coincided with your dream? It is perfectly possible also for loved ones in the next dimension to communicate with you, but it is certainly the exception rather than the rule.

Eileen Garrett is another extraordinary medium studied by many leading scientific bodies. Sir Oliver Lodge, one of the world's foremost physicists, was absolutely convinced that he had communicated with his son, who had died in the First World War. These dialogues were reported in his book entitled *Raymond,* published in 1916.

Some of the great scientists who have contributed to psychical research are as follows: Henry Sidgwick, Edmund Gurney, Professor William James (called the father of American psychology), Sir William Crookes, Arthur Conan Doyle, and J. B. Rhine. Myers of Cambridge published *Human Personality and Its Survival of Bodily Death,* a universally acknowledged masterpiece.

It is true, mind can communicate with mind, and we must learn to differentiate between communication from our subconscious mind and that of a loved one. Do not seek guidance from men or women either on this plane or the next dimension. They do it through psychic perception. Follow the injunction of the Bible, which says: *If any of you lack wisdom, let him ask of God, that giveth to all men liberally, and upbraideth not; and it shall be given him* (James 1:5).

POINTS TO REMEMBER

1. There are two phases of your mind. One is called the conscious mind, which chooses, rationalizes, analyzes, and reasons inductively and deductively.

The other is your subconscious mind which only reasons deductively. It is the seat of memory, emotion, clairvoyance, clairaudience, and telepathy. Infinite intelligence and boundless wisdom reside in your subconscious mind. Whatever your conscious mind conveys to your subconscious, the latter accepts, whether it is true or false.

2. Your subconscious mind does not look at two ideas and then make a decision as to which is best. You are to decide that with your conscious mind.

3. When you are hypnotized, your subconscious mind will accept the suggestion of the operator without question. For example, if you are told you are a dog, you will play the part of a dog to the best of your ability. You will bark when you are told to do so and you will lap up milk like a dog.

4. Your subconscious mind is amenable to suggestion and is controlled by suggestion. For instance, if a person believes in devils or evil spirits and in a hypnotic trance it is suggested to him that he is possessed by devils, he will dramatize and exhibit the roles of as many devils as are embraced in the suggestion. In other words, his subconscious accepts the suggestion. Subjective hallucinations of devils with hooves and horns, tails with stings, wings of a bat, and other horrendous monitions and shapes appear, all of which are figments of his distorted, twisted superstitions and beliefs which his subconscious dredges up to conform to his beliefs. A man who never heard of devils and did not believe in such teachings would not have any such experience.

5. If you say to a hypnotized person who believes in a heaven up there somewhere and who believes that there are angels and golden thrones and celestial choirs, "You are in heaven now," he will become peaceful, loving, and ecstatic and describe what he

believes to be heaven. His subconscious, accepting the suggestion, dramatizes his childhood belief and picture of heaven. He doesn't know that he is in heaven now, which is his own mind and spirit.

6. If you give a glass of water to a hypnotized subject and tell him it is whiskey, he will become intoxicated and play the role of a drunkard. The reason is his subconscious takes your suggestion literally and acts accordingly.

7. If, prior to being hypnotized, you give yourself a powerful auto-suggestion that you will not do anything ridiculous or contrary to your moral code, the suggestion of the operator that you disrobe or steal will prove to be of no avail because your subconscious accepts your dominant suggestion. The stronger suggestion always prevails.

8. If you suggest to yourself boldly and meaningfully that no one can hypnotize you, it follows automatically that you can't be hypnotized by the operator. You simply close your mind to his suggestion and tune in on the Infinite within you, and then you are immune.

9. In the waking state you can always reject the suggestions of others by thinking on whatsoever things are true, lovely, noble, and God-like.

10. It is dangerous to practice automatic (psychic) writing if you are afraid of evil spirits, discarnate entities, or guides in the astral realm. You attract what you fear, and when you suggest fear to your subconscious and feel guilty and resentful toward others, you open up the psychic doors of your mind and dredge up all the debris from your subconscious. When you feel guilty, it is always accompanied by fear and expectation of punishment, and your subconscious, reacting according to the suggestions given it (namely, fear, guilt, resent-

ment, etc.), proceeds to talk to you, oftentimes in blasphemous language, disturbing you mentally and physically. Actually, it is a playback of the contents of your own subconscious mind.

11. The way to overcome the hearing of voices and the belief that you are possessed by evil entities which urge you to commit suicide and all manner of evil is to realize that when you fill your mind with the truths of God, you neutralize and obliterate all these negative patterns. The best prayer to use is the protective 91st Psalm. Read it over slowly, quietly, and feelingly many times a day. These spiritual vibrations will be conveyed to your subconscious mind and will destroy, annihilate, and cleanse all dirty linen in the closet of your mind. When fear and negative voices come to your mind, affirm immediately: "God's love fills my soul." Keep it up and after a while you will be free.

12. A woman asked the ouija board, "Who is writing the message?" The answer was, "Only you." In other words, her subconscious mind was operating the ouija board, supplying whatever kind of message she wished to hear; her subconscious, being governed by suggestion, acted accordingly. Had she believed in discarnate entities or that departed loved ones were operating the ouija board and responding to her, her subconscious mind, being true to its nature, would have played the role of an imaginary departed relative.

13. It is possible to take even a streetwalker who has little or no education and who knows nothing about Eastern philosophy, Oriental religions, or immortality, and hypnotize her to activate her psychic perception in the presence of men and women who are thoroughly versed in these subjects. When potent suggestions are given to her, such as

"You are now a priestess in the Temple of the Sun; you will give a marvelous disquisition on Oriental philosophy; you are very wise, learned etc.," her appearance changes and she assumes a regal posture and gives a marvelous lecture. Her subconscious acts upon the suggestion given and taps the subconscious mind of all present, and her discourse is simply a composite of their beliefs and assumptions. In the trance state, she could also receive data on these subjects from the treasury or storehouse of the universal subconscious.

14. There are many self-styled mediums who profess to get in touch with loved ones in the next dimension of life. You can go to one and give your name, such as Mary Jones, and ask for a message. The medium assumes it is a sister or mother in the next dimension, but you have no sister or mother there. You receive a very comforting, loving message purporting to be from your loved one. All this is due to the suggestion of the medium to her subconscious mind, and it answers accordingly. The same medium will give you a comforting message from an imaginary or non-existent person, also.

15. There are outstanding mediums who undoubtedly do receive communications from the next dimension of life; among them are Arthur Ford, Eileen Garrett, and the late Geraldine Cummins, who was investigated by a great number of scientific bodies. She has been acclaimed by the Psychical Research Society of England.

16. I believe the late Bishop Pike's dialogues with his son through the mediumship of Arthur Ford were definitely genuine, fourth-dimensional communications between father and son.

17. If you hypnotized a man and suggested to him he was your brother but he had never met your

brother, he would be incapable of assuming his gestures, demeanor, diction, tonal qualities, or mannerisms. He would play an imaginary role, but it would not be that of your brother. He could not impersonate your brother because his subconscious had no memory of your brother.

16

How to Let Psychic Perception
Work for You and Your Children

The Book of Proverbs 13:24 says: *He that spareth his rod hateth his son: but he that loveth him chasteneth him betimes.* Proverbs 23:13 and 29:15: *Withhold not correction from the child: for if thou beatest him with the rod, he shall not die. Thou shalt beat him with the rod, and shalt deliver his soul from hell. The rod and reproof give wisdom: but a child left to himself bringeth his mother to shame.*

These are marvelous words of wisdom for parents today. The modern-day custom of permissiveness and generally letting the child do what he wants to do without correction and discipline is disastrous. Every child needs discipline and correction. You must express your disapproval when a small boy hits his sister or breaks her dolls. Let him know in no uncertain terms that he is not allowed to do this.

Children can be little animals. They may want to run wild and not go to school; you may have to take them by the ear and see to it that they do go to school and behave. *There is no love without discipline and no discipline without love.*

He that spareth the rod hateth. . . "Hate" in the Bible means to reject the negatives, such as impudence, lying,

disorderly conduct, stealing, etc. Keep in mind the fact that
we are dealing with the language of the 16th century. *Except
a man hate his father. . .* doesn't mean you hate your father.
It means to reject his beliefs of hell, of an angry God, and of
superstitious beliefs. *He that loveth his son chasteneth. . .*
means that the father disciplines his son or his daughter and
makes the child conform to the Golden Rule and the law of
love.

A child has to be taught manners, deportment, sharing,
cooperation, respect for authority, respect for parents, and
prayer therapy. *Withhold not correction from the child: for
if thou beatest him with the rod, he shall not die.* He shall
not die to love, peace, harmony, right action, honesty,
respect for others and their property, and reverence for
things Divine. "I die daily," Paul says; that is, die to ill will,
bitterness, and false beliefs.

Honor thy father and mother. If a boy doesn't honor his
parents, how can he respect his teachers, professors, policemen, and others in authority? *Wisdom is justified of her
children.* Wisdom is awareness of the power of God. There
are "children" of the mind, also, such as books, plays,
paintings, buildings, songs, music, and shows. When you look
at the cesspool of iniquity displayed on some book stalls, you
realize they must come forth from twisted, distorted, and
disturbed personalities—which, to say the least, is putting it
mildly.

If you had a deep reverence for the Supreme Architect,
what kind of paintings would you bring forth? Since you
would be in tune with the indescribable beauty of God, you
would bring forth things of beauty and joy forever. In this
light, think of the art of Michaelangelo.

*Thou shalt beat him with the rod, and shalt deliver his
soul from hell.* "Hell" means restriction, self-imposed bondage, misery, and suffering—all brought on by poisoning and
polluting our subconscious mind with hatred, resentment,
hostility, and bigotry; but when the child is taught the real

meaning of the Ten Commandments, the Golden Rule, and the wholesome use of his mind, and is properly guided to conform when he is young, he will grow up and acquire the habit of filling his mind with life-giving patterns.

The rod and reproof give wisdom. When you have wisdom, you coordinate all your activities in Divine order. You are capable of tuning in on the Infinite Intelligence within you and receiving answers to the most perplexing problems. "Divine order" means that you express yourself at your highest level, and you radiate love and goodwill to all. Having wisdom, you know that to hate, resent, or to be envious of another, you simply poison your soul and mind and bring all manner of diseases, mental and physical, upon yourself.

A child left to himself bringeth his mother to shame. This means that a child left to wander off without spiritual instruction and without ordinary rules of good conduct will grow up with a contaminated mind, will perhaps become a delinquent, and possibly will even end up in jail.

I have visited some boys' clubs, and met with Boy Scouts, DeMolays, and others, and they are remarkable boys, clean and wholesome, with respect for their parents. They also want to contribute to the harmony, beauty, and welfare of their country. They want to be, to do, to have, and to serve. They realize that they must change themselves, and that by reforming themselves they will help to reform the world.

You will perceive the wisdom, true knowledge, and understanding of parents in the lives, actions, and reactions of their sons and daughters. The children, as the Bible mentions, "justify" the wisdom of their parents. To justify means to fit exactly; mentally, it means that the children reflect accurately the wise indoctrination of their parents. Action by the parents and the reaction of the children are equal. Their wisdom, which represents knowledge of the laws of mind, and the response of Infinite Spirit, are definitely, positively, and absolutely reflected in their mental attitudes, in their studies, and in their accomplishments and achievements in life.

When the wisdom of God is enthroned in the minds of youth, the result is balance, equilibrium, harmony, peace, right action, and happiness. The boy's work equates with his state of mind. The inside and the outside are balanced, or "justified."

Teach your children to pray for Divine guidance by claiming it boldly, and the impulse will always be lifeward, upward, and Godward. The law of correspondence, or parallels, is always working. All of us, including boys and girls, get the result which corresponds to our habitual thinking and imagery.

This is what an outstanding educator, Mr. William H. Thrall, has to say:

"I am a sort of an old-fashioned educator, and I have administered my share of corporal punishment in my day. I applied this treatment judiciously, and in every case it seemed to be of value to the pupil concerned.

"I cannot help being acquainted with many of the permissive parents, because there are so many of them. They are shocked and saddened when they learn that their offspring is in jail, is pregnant without a husband, is on dope, or is dead from dope. I am saddened for them, and I have known them all, but in many cases wise corporal punishment and a sincere religious atmosphere might have prevented the tragedy.

"Corporal punishment and religion are basic parts of the British school system, and when I was employed by the British, I saw no hippies, sloppy dress, drug addiction, or lack of respect for authority."

Boy Says Father Is Too Easy-Going

A young boy about 11 years of age, who was making trouble in school, insulting the teacher, and stealing from other children, was whipped by his father with a strap. Afterwards, his father said to him, "Son, I'm sorry. I shouldn't have whipped you."

The little boy said, "I deserved it, and I don't know why he said he was sorry."

The boy knew he was wrong and deserved the punishment, and it was very foolish for the father to talk to his son that way. Presumably, the father thought his son would love him less because he disciplined him. On the contrary, the father showed his interest in the welfare of his son by punishing him. Actually, he demonstrated his love in the sense that he wanted his son to grow up to be honest, upright, and a good student. No boy resents being punished when he knows he deserves it.

I might add that when a father or mother disciplines a child, the parent is, in effect, saying, "I love you. I am interested in your future. I want you to grow up to be a man of integrity, justice, and honesty, a man whom your co-workers, neighbors, and employers will respect because of your contribution to society. I am just endeavoring to instruct you to conduct yourself in an acceptable way, because one of these days I am going on to the next dimension of life and will not be around to watch over you and advise you. Remember, if you cheat, rob, and insult others, society will not forgive you and you will discover that you will be punished for your misdeeds."

Let Psychic Perception Raise Your Child

Your perception of the truth that God indwells every child gives you the opportunity to constantly claim that the wisdom, intelligence, harmony, and love of God are resurrected in your offspring. You are always *en rapport* subconsciously with your child, and the latter feels your conviction and responds accordingly. You are living in an objective and subjective world, and you must also do those things which are objectively correct.

Why Permissiveness Is Always Wrong

Permissive parents do not really understand the laws of their conscious and subconscious mind. Children learn by education, observation, and experience. Parents should control their children, teach them about God and the powers within them in a very simple way so the child can understand. Children should never be permitted to do as they like, but must definitely be taught and made to conform to the Golden Rule and think, speak, and act towards others as they would wish others to think, speak, and act towards them. When parents do not correct and discipline their children, or offer proper guidance, the latter lack self-reliance, security, and self-control. Parents must exercise their authority and discipline with rationality, understanding, love, and responsiveness to the child. When they do, their children grow up full of self-confidence, poise, balance, and self-control. These parents issue sound directives and instructions to their children and they point out to them why their commands are right. They are able to explain lucidly to the children why the directives are for their good.

Avoid the Dictatorial, Authoritarian, and Totalitarian Attitude

Recently I talked to a young girl of 18, who said her mother had laid the law down to her in no uncertain terms, with orders such as: "Keep away from all boys; sex is evil; men are beasts like your father. You can't use rouge or lipstick or powder—these are of the devil; you must not dance or go to the movies—all these are sins; you must believe in our religion—if you don't, you will burn in a lake of fire," etc.

This mother was really a little Hitler with her you-must-do-this-or-else attitude. The girl was full of fear; she was frustrated, hateful, discontented, and suffering from a profound inferiority complex. She came from New England, and as you probably have surmised already, she had run away from home.

The first thing I did was to teach her who she was from a spiritual standpoint by explaining that there was only one Power and Presence, and that It was within her. I further explained to her that she could contact this Supreme Intelligence and It would respond to her and guide, direct, and prosper her beyond her fondest dreams.

The Special Prayer

The following is the prayer technique I suggested for her:

> I am wanted, I am loved, I am needed, I am appreciated, I am Divinely expressed. I forgive myself for harboring resentful thoughts, and I fully and freely forgive my mother. Whenever I think of her, I will affirm, 'God's love fills your soul.' I am at peace. I am joyous, happy, and free. I am gainfully employed. I have a wonderful income consistent with integrity and honesty. I know that as I repeat these ideas, they sink down into my subconscious, and according to the law of my mind (as I sow, so shall I reap), all these truths will come to pass.

This young girl made a habit of this prayer, and in time it completely transformed her life. She now has a wonderful office position and is bubbling over with the joy of living.

She Asked, "Why Aren't My Parents Happy?"

A young girl of 14 was sent to talk with me by her parents. She was getting very poor grades in school, hated certain subjects, and her teacher reported to the parents that she could do much better but that she seemed to have no interest or motivation. She said to me that she supposed her parents would get a divorce, as they were always quarrelling and saying nasty things to each other. Then she asked, "Why aren't my parents happy?"

In talking with the parents, I pointed out that there was no one to change but themselves and that there was no question but that their daughter was mentally and emotionally affected by the turmoil and bitterness in the home. They agreed to spend five or six minutes every morning alternating with Psalms: 1, 23, 27, 91, and 100. After meditating on one of these Psalms every morning, they contemplated the Presence of God in their daughter, claiming that the wisdom, intelligence, harmony, and beauty of the Infinite were now being resurrected in her life. They both pictured her telling them about her wonderful success in school. They imagined her smiling, radiant, and happy.

At the end of a month's time, this young girl became one of the finest students in the school. Her manners, deportment, and outlook on life thrilled her parents and made them very happy.

This is to remind all parents that children grow in the image and likeness of the dominant mental and spiritual atmosphere of the home. As parents contemplate the Presence of God in their children, they will not be worried or fearful about their welfare and protection. The parents who commune with the indwelling God-Presence every day, claiming harmony, peace, beauty, inspiration, and guidance, have marriages which grow more blessed through the years, and the rich spiritual atmosphere in the home will impinge on the subconscious mind of their children.

You Must Possess a Psychic Insight into the Power of Your Words

Parents must never say to their children: "You're no good, you will never amount to anything, you are stupid, you're dumb, you're a bad boy, etc." All these words are thoughts expressed, and the boys' or girls' minds, being very impressionable, are receptive to these thoughts. The children accept these thoughts subconsciously, and proceed to react accordingly. The little boy begins to think he is stupid and dumb when, in reality, he is not. Oftentimes he fights back by being delinquent, troublesome, and hostile. There is no use in saying to the boy that he is stupid in addition and substraction since he doesn't know the answers. The only thing to do is to teach him.

It is futile and foolish to denounce and condemn a pail of dirty water. The solution would be to pour clean water in, even if it is drop by drop. After a reasonable period of time, you will have a pail of clean water. Likewise, parents should teach their children in a simple way that God is all-wise, that He knows all things, and that He will always respond to them. Teach them to ask God for guidance in their studies with the confidence that He can solve every problem for them. The young person can easily understand that God is the life-principle within him and that he does not see God or life; neither does he see his thoughts, his mind, nor his love for his dog, all of which represent God in him.

One boy of 12, who regularly attends my lectures on Sunday mornings, once said to his mother as he arrived home, "Mom, I know where God is. God is within me. I can't see God, but I can feel love, joy, happiness, and that is God moving in me. I can't see the wind, Mom, but I can feel the breeze upon my face." There are many ways you can teach boys or girls about the God-Presence within them, such as listening to a beautiful symphony, yet pointing out that they don't see the players. Show them that they may turn on the light, but that they don't see electricity.

How to Keep God Alive in Your Home

Have regular morning and evening prayers in which the children join. Teach the children to offer grace at mealtime and remind your boys and girls frequently that God created all things—the stars, the sun, the moon, and the whole world, and that when they love each other, they are expressing God's love. Teach them that God is the Infinite Healing Presence that heals a cut on their finger and gives them new skin when they burn themselves.

Young boys and girls going to school become enthusiastic when I explain to them that if they practice a simple technique every night they will be guided in their studies and pass all their examinations easily and in a relaxed manner. The following is the simple prayer that great numbers of young boys and girls, as well as those going to college, use regularly every night before going to sleep:

> I am Divinely guided in my studies, and I have a perfect memory for everything I need to know at every moment of time and point of space. I pass all examinations in Divine order. Whatever my study assignments may be, I will give attention to them, and I know my subconscious will prompt me and reveal to me the answers when I need them. I sleep in peace and I wake in joy.

Pass on this prayer technique to your sons and daughters and explain to them that these simple truths, when repeated regularly for five or six minutes every night, are engraved in their subconscious mind, which is the seat of memory; and whatever is impressed on their subconscious will be expressed. In other words, tell tl em that they will be compelled to give a good account of themselves at every examination, for the nature of the subconscious is compulsive.

A Young Girl of 12 Talks to God and Solves Her Problem

A niece of mine studying in a convent in England wrote me stating that when the sister in charge told her that she could do much better than she was doing, and after reflecting on her studies, she decided to talk to God about it. Her prayer was very simple and practical. Her dialogue was like this:

"God, You are all wise; guide me and show me how to give my best in every way. Thank you, God." She expected an answer and received one and is now getting along famously with the teachers and her schoolmates and in her studies.

Remember, the nature of this Supreme Intelligence within you is responsiveness, and the simple prayer from the heart always gets an answer. Teaching children the Presence and Power of God is as necessary as food and vitamins, clothing, and shelter. It is the living bread from heaven.

A Plan for Parents and Children

Parents should remember that they can give only what they have or possess in their minds; therefore, parents should learn the laws of the mind and the ways of the Infinite Intelligence within all people throughout the world. Let this be your creed:

> God is, and all there is is God, in all, over all, through all, and all in all. God is the Living Spirit, the Life-Principle within each one. God loves us and cares for us. God comes first in our lives. As we turn to this Infinite Presence and Power within us and claim harmony, peace, abundance, wisdom, right action, and beauty operating in our lives, wonders happen as we pray this way.

> Every morning when we open our eyes, we give thanks to God for the new day and for the marvelous opportunities to release more and more of His light, love, truth, and beauty to all mankind. Every night before we go to sleep, we will say, "We

sleep in peace and we wake in joy, and we live in God. God gives his beloved in sleep."

The above prayer, recited regularly, systematically, and persistently by parents in the presence of their children will resurrect and activate these truths lodged in the subconscious of all. Children brought up in this spiritual radiance will grow in wisdom, truth, and beauty, and will prove the age-old dictum that the only reason for our existence is to glorify God and enjoy Him forever.

POINTS TO REMEMBER

1. Every child needs discipline and correction. You must express your disapproval when he doesn't conform to universally accepted standards in the home, school, or wherever he may be. *There is no love without discipline and no discipline without love.*

2. The word "hate" in the Bible means to reject completely and emphatically the negatives of life, such as lying, disorderly conduct, stealing, etc. In other words, you never condone that which is wrong. You must see to it that the child learns his lesson, and when he does, he will not be a repeater.

3. Wisdom is justified of her children. There are "children" also, such as books, plays, paintings, songs, etc. All these reflect the state of mind of the creative individual.

4. When a child is taught the real meaning of the Ten Commandments and the Golden Rule, he will incorporate these truths into his mentality and reveal Divine law and order in his life.

5. A child left to wander off without spiritual instruction will grow up confused and truculent.

6. Children justify the wisdom of their parents. This

means that the children reflect accurately the wise indoctrination of their parents.

7. Children know when they deserve punishment; they know they had it coming. A father who disciplines his son is actually revealing his love for him, as he shows his interest in his future and in his welfare.

8. As parents regularly identify with the God-Presence in the child and claim that the wisdom, intelligence, and harmony of God are being expressed by the child, such a child will grow in grace, beauty, and wisdom in perception.

9. Permissive parents who are negligent and careless and don't control, direct, and make certain requirements of their children through psychic perception have children who lack self-confidence, security, self-control, and who are also selfish.

10. Parents who are quarreling and generally exhibiting hostility to each other communicate subconsciously these negative vibrations to their children, which disturb them and cause them to feel they are not loved or appreciated. Furthermore, they become fearful of a broken home and lose that sense of security so needed in their formative years. Sometimes they show their retaliation in acts of stealing, poor study records, indifference, and a generally rebellious attitude.

11. Children at an early age can begin to perceive and understand God. You can point out that God is their mind, their life, and that this Presence watches over them as they sleep; that It heals, inspires and guides them in their studies. The little boy or girl can understand that he or she can't see the wind, but can feel the breeze upon the face; likewise, he or she can feel love, joy, and laughter, all of which are of God.

12. Boys and girls going to school can get acquainted

with the Infinite Intelligence within them by affirming for five or six minutes every night: "Infinite Intelligence guides me in my studies, and I have a perfect memory for everything I need to know at all times. I pass all examinations in Divine order." They will experience the result of what they sow in their mind. This is one way of getting acquainted with the God-Presence within them.

13. A young girl of 12 talks with psychic perception to God and requests that He guide her in her studies, and she goes ahead by leaps and bounds.

17

How to Let Psychic Perception
Make Your Desires Come True

It is all right to have a dream, an ideal, or a goal, but you must have a solid foundation under your aspirations; otherwise they become idle fantasy, which wastes your energy and debilitates your entire organism. There are many men and women who do not know where they are going and who have not risen above their childhood dreams. Somehow their fantasies become enmeshed and confused with reality, and they have difficulty in differentiating one from the other. Hence their need for using their psychic perception.

**How She Made Her Dream a Reality
by Calling on Her Subconscious Mind**

Some months ago, I interviewed a young woman in Las Vegas, Nevada. On my return to that city, where I am writing this chapter, she visited me to tell me how she had made her dream come true.

On her first interview with me, she said that she was constantly daydreaming about being a movie star, with valets, servants, limousines, maids, and butlers at her command. Yet she admitted she had no talents along the line of acting. She was emotionally immature and had simply carried over into her adult life a childish image of being a famous movie princess. She had had numerous affairs with men, each of whom had promised her a movie career, but she inevitably discovered that they were simply using her, which resulted in frustration and complete disillusionment on her part.

I suggested that she now use constructively the talents she had. She could type very well. Also, her ability at shorthand was excellent. I pointed out to her at that first interview that she should come down to earth and be practical and cease dwelling in marble mansions in the sky. I suggested that she affirm as follows: "Infinite Intelligence opens up the perfect door for my full expression, where I am giving of my talents in a wonderful way and I am Divinely compensated. I claim I am wanted, needed, loved, and cherished by a wonderful husband, and I contribute to his success and happiness in a wonderful way." I explained to her that as she repeated these affirmations, they would sink down into her subconscious mind, and the deeper currents of her subconscious would bring her desires to pass.

A Clear-Cut Lead Came into Her Mind

Subsequently, this young lady attended a social gathering in Las Vegas and there met a professor of English, who asked her to become his secretary. She is now married to him and is extremely happy. The lead that came to her was a deep, almost compelling psychic impulse to attend the social function for which she had previously turned down an invitation. The wisdom of her subconscious perceptive mind knew how to fulfill her dreams and bring them to pass. She is no longer building castles in the air. She knows how to construct a foundation under them.

How Dave Built a Solid Foundation

Today I had dinner with an old friend, Dave, who directs a most progressive and enlightened congregation. One Sunday morning many years ago, Dave came to one of my lectures at the Wilshire Ebell Theatre, Los Angeles. He became intensely interested in the teaching and shortly thereafter became chief usher in the organization where he remained for many years. Dave had been in the musical theatrical field and had degrees along these lines, but he was dissatisfied and frustrated in his efforts to rise above just making ends meet.

I suggested to Dave that inasmuch as he was wildly enthusiastic about the inner meaning of the Bible and the workings of the subconscious mind, I believed he would be a tremendous success in the ministerial field. This idea rang a bell in Dave's subjective mind, and he took the five years of training necessary to become a minister of Religious Science. He became an instantaneous success for the simple reason that he is now doing what he loves to do and is Divinely happy and Divinely prospered. He fell heir to one of the most beautiful churches in the state, following the resignation of its chief pastor. He now conducts youth programs, Science of Mind classes twice weekly, and Sunday morning lectures. His organization is growing by leaps and bounds.

He told me that he has never been so happy in his life, and he is extraordinarily successful in his work in Las Vegas.

His Foundation Technique

During his ministerial training, every night prior to sleep he would sit still, immobilize his attention, and imagine that he was standing on a pulpit expounding the great truths of God to an imaginary audience. He felt the reality of this so much that before he was ordained, he said to me, "I am absolutely convinced that I will have my own church and be the pastor. I sense it, feel it, and in a vision I have seen the church and congregation about 100 times." And all this came to pass, thus proving what Thoreau had said many years ago: "If any man will hold a picture in his mind of doing what he wants to do and will sustain that mental picture, the God-Power will develop it and bring it to pass."

You, too, can build a real solid foundation under your heart's desire. Dave said to me today that he stresses to his own students that their castles in the air without a basic knowledge of the powers of the subconscious to bring them into being are as unsubstantial as whiffs of smoke.

His Reversed Attitude in Perception Brought Him Assets of a Quarter of a Million Dollars

I had a most interesting session with a man whom we shall call Mr. X, who has been phoning and corresponding with me for some time. I gave him spiritual advice over the phone, and the following is the history of the case. He is the son of a very wealthy father in the East, who had been very cruel and autocratic, insisting that the son come up to his standards in the business. This young man had a neurotic hatred for his father and began to strike back by writing vitriolic articles about big business; moreover, he went back East and lectured on the values of a communistic society to a club to which his father belonged, knowing that this would infuriate his father. His desire, as he said, was to strike back at his father. In the meantime, because of this emotional hostility and suppressed rage, plus his sense of guilt, he began to drink excessively, becoming an inebriate, or compulsive drinker. He also developed ulcers and high blood pressure; and, as if that were not enough, he was on the verge of bankruptcy.

My explanation (over the phone) of the reason for his actions supplied 75 percent of his cure. He realized that he was being emotionally immature and was consuming alcohol to assuage his sense of guilt just as someone else would take aspirin for a headache. Actually, it suddenly dawned on him that he was literally destroying himself by attempting to hit back at his father's ideals and policies. He decided to reverse his attitude by following the technique of scientific prayer.

He affirmed out loud frequently during the day: "I surrender my father to God. I release him completely and wish for him health, peace, success, and all the blessings of life. Whenever I think of him, I will affirm at once, 'I have released you. God's peace fills your soul.' I am Divinely guided. Divine law and order govern me. Divine love and Divine peace saturate my soul. My food and drink are God's ideas, which constantly unfold within me, bringing me harmony, health, and peace. God thinks, speaks and acts through me, and I am Divinely expressed and fulfilled in all ways."

He repeated these truths frequently out loud, which prevented his mind from wandering. Whenever any negative thoughts came to his mind, he would affirm: "God loves me and cares for me." After a few weeks, he became a constructive thinker.

His "Movie" Technique

Every night for about ten minutes in a perfectly relaxed state, he imagined I was in front of him congratulating him on his freedom from alcohol, and whenever the shakes and the jitters seized him with the craving for another drink, he would cause to flash in his mind the mental movie, knowing there was an Almighty Power backing him up. It was only a matter of a few weeks until he was completely free from the curse of compulsive drinking. His new attitude changed everything. Today, three months later, at dinner with me in Las Vegas, he told me his business has prospered so well hat his assets are worth over $200,000. His psychic perception had enabled him to make the correct ana shrewd decisions necessary in accumulating a fortune.

His Facial Tic Was Ruining His Career

During a trip to Mexico and its famous pyramids, I met a minister who had a pronounced facial tic which was very aggravating and humiliating to him. He had received alcoholic injections, which were supposed to deaden or paralyze the nerve, but after some months the tic flared up again. The condition became very acute when he spoke before his congregation or other social gatherings. He had reached the point where he was actually contemplating resigning because of the comments of the people and his own sense of embarrassment.

After a prolonged discussion, however, I remarked that I had a deep inner feeling that he had a pronounced sense of hurt plus a guilt complex which he was unwilling to face subjectively and objectively. This tic condition was affecting his right eye, which could possibly symbolize something he did not want to look at in his home or office; there was some reason why his subconscious was selecting his face and his right eye as a scapegoat. This situation needed his psychic perception to recognize how to deal with it.

He admitted freely that he no longer believed in what he was teaching, which gave him a guilt complex; moreover, he was afraid to resign because he felt he could not make a living outside the ministry. He deeply resented members of his board, who criticized whenever he deviated from the ortho- dox standard of teaching. All this nervous pressure was converted by his subconscious mind into a tic. The affliction compensated him in a morbid way for his failure to be honest and forthright and admit to his congregation that he no longer believed according to the directives and dogma of the church.

He freely admitted all this to me, and I suggested to him in turn that on the following Sunday when he returned from his vacation he should speak freely from the platform and tell his congregation that he was resigning, since he no longer believed what he was preaching. He understood that to teach one thing and to believe another created a powerful negative conflict in his mind, resulting in mental and physical disorder.

He spoke from the depths of his heart to his congregation and then resigned. In a letter to me he said, "I felt a tremendous relief and a great sense of peace came over me. My constant affirmation was, 'Thou wilt show me the path of life,' and one of my former board members gave me a position as personnel director for his organization, where I am happy." He added, "What you said is true. Oftentimes the explanation is the cure."

If you have a problem, mental, physical, or emotional, ask yourself: "What am I turning away from? What is it I don't want to face? Am I hiding my resentment and hostility to someone?" Face the problem and solve it with psychic perception, dissolve it in the light of God's love.

She Didn't Have to Be Lonely

I once conducted a seminar at sea on the ship *Princess Carla,* which visited several ports in Mexico. I also conducted daily lectures and personal interviews. A young woman from New York City, although not a member of our seminar, interviewed me because she had read *The Power of Your Subconscious Mind.* * The substance of her conversation was that she was always attracting the wrong men. They were either alcoholics, married, or individuals suffering from sex deviation complexes. She was somewhat withdrawn, hostile, and on the defensive. I asked her a very simple question: "What's eating you inside?" adding that is what the Kahuna (a Hawaiian priest) always asks a person who visits him for a healing. She blurted out, "I hate my mother. When my

---

*Dr. Joseph Murphy, *The Power of Your Subconscious Mind* (Englewood Cliffs, N.J.: Prentice-Hall, Inc., 1963).

brother died of scarlet fever, my mother said to me, 'Why wasn't it you?' "

This was a terrific shock to the impressionable mind of a 13-year-old girl. Undoubtedly the mother in the anguish of grief didn't really mean what she said when she reproached the girl because she, the only daughter, lived instead of her brother. This young lady, very attractive and charming, had met many men on the cruise but was very critical of every one of them. She had what you might call a rejection complex, as she lived in the fear that she could not be loved. She expected to be rejected, not realizing that what she feared would always be made manifest. Underneath she was hungry for companionship and wanted passionately to be appreciated, wanted, and loved. Her subconscious conflict stemmed back to her mother's critical remark, "Why wasn't it you?"

We had a long chat in my cabin on the ship and I pointed out to her that the past was dead and that nothing mattered but this moment; that all she had to do was to change her present thoughts and keep them changed, and her future would be a perfect projection of her new habitual thinking, based on the premise that what we sow in the garden of our mind, so shall we reap in our experience. Accordingly, I outlined a pattern of affirmations for her, explaining to her that she must never deny what she affirmed. The affirmation was as follows:

> I know that the past is dead, and all I have to do is to fill my subconscious mind with life-giving patterns of thought, and all the negative and traumatic hurts of the past will be obliterated. I claim now that Infinite Intelligence is guiding and directing me, and that Divine love fills my soul. I am inspired and illumined, and my hidden talents are revealed to me. I radiate love, peace, and goodwill to all men and women. I have much to

give to man. I am honest, sincere; I appreciate a lovely home. I can cherish, love, and admire a man who has a reverence for things Divine. I love a beautiful home, I am economical and I can contribute in a wonderful way to a man who is also loving, kind, and peaceful. Whenever I think of my mother, I bless her. She is now in the next dimension of life and I claim her journey is ever onward, upward, and Godward. I forgive myself for harboring resentful thoughts, and I know God loves me and cares for me. Whenever I am prone to criticize myself, I will immediately affirm, 'God loves me and cares for me.'

I was pleasantly surpised when this young lady came to my lecture a few Sundays ago and introduced me to her husband, a retired captain of the British Navy. They are extremely happy and are now on a world cruise, which will last about eight months. She had absorbed these truths we discussed in her subconscious mind. As she said, it was one hour of perception that transformed her life. It is true that you can be changed in the twinkling of an eye.

POINTS TO REMEMBER

1. It is all right to have a dream, but you must have a solid psychic foundation under the dream; otherwise, it becomes but idle fantasy.

2. Learn what your talents are now, face yourself as to your present capabilities, and start from there; then realize that you are Divinely guided to your true expression and Divinely compensated in a wonderful way. The answer will come from your subconscious mind, and you will recognize the lead, which comes to you clearly and distinctly.

3. If you hold a picture in your mind of what you want

to be and dramatize it in your imagination, knowing that your subconscious mind will develop it and bring it to pass, and as you remain faithful to this mental picture, the way will open up and you will become that which you imagined and felt as true.

4. You actually tend to destroy yourself physically and mentally by striking back at others or by seeking revenge. The answer is to release them to God, wishing for them all the blessings of life. If you are an alcoholic, forgive yourself for harboring negative thoughts and imagine some friend congratulating you on your freedom and peace of mind. As you continue to project this mental movie, your subconscious will take over and compel you to lose all desire or craving for alcohol. The law of your subconscious is compulsion, and whatever you impress upon it is expressed. You can control its compulsions with your psychic perception.

5. A facial tic can be due to a deep-seated resentment plus a guilt complex and an unwillingness to face the conflict boldly and overcome it. The thing to do is to face it objectively with psychic perception in your own mind and be honest with yourself by refusing to believe and teach what you know and feel in your heart is not true. Claim that Infinite Intelligence within you opens up a new door of expression for you, and It will respond to you in Divine order, and a desired healing will follow.

6. When a woman hates her mother and dwells on old hurts and psychic traumas, she will attract to herself the wrong type of men, based on the law that like attracts like. The thing for her to do is to realize that the past is dead; nothing lives but this moment. As she changes her present thought, she will change the future, since her future is her present thoughts made manifest.

18

The Psychic Perception
of Your Past Lives

Emerson said, "There is one mind common to all individual men. Every man is an inlet to the same and to all of the same. He that is once admitted to the right of reason is made a freeman of the whole estate. What Plato has taught, he may think; what a saint has felt, he may feel; what at any time has befallen man, he can understand. Who hath access to this universal mind is a party to all that is or can be done, for this is the only and sovereign agent."

This means that your subconscious mind, which is one with the universal subjective mind of the entire human race, possesses a memory of everything that has ever transpired in the evolution of man, both physiologically and mentally. All the languages ever spoken, all the music of the world, plus the discoveries, inventions, and experiences of all men are registered indelibly and infallibly in your subconscious mind. This chapter will discuss psychic perception of this storehouse of human experience.

Your Subconscious Reasons Deductively Only

Your subconscious does not argue controversially. It

accepts the premise (true or false) given it by your conscious mind and reasons deductively from that premise to all legitimate inferences, with a marvelous clarity and accuracy.

An Interesting Hypnotic Experiment Regarding Past Lives

Some time ago I witnessed an experiment conducted by a friend of mine on a man we will call Mr. X. He was a Roman Catholic and disbelieved violently in reincarnation; however, the psychologist said to him that if he put him into a trance, he would tape his answers and prove to him that he had had many past lives. In the hypnotic state, the psychologist suggested to Mr. X that he was now taking him back 500 years ago, and Mr. X was to inform him who he was, where he was living, and what he was doing. There was no response. The psychologist then said, "It is 1,000 years ago. Who are you? What's your name?" There was no reply. Then in desperation the psychologist said to Mr. X, "I am now regressing you way back, long before England or Ireland were ever heard of—way, way back. Who are you?"

There was silence for about a minute, then Mr. X said, "On the seventh day I rested."

This ended the hypnotic experiment on reincarnation with Mr. X.

The Reason for the Failure

It is generally true that in the hypnotic trance state, you will always give the operator what he wants; i.e., you will cooperate with him. Assuming the correctness of the premise, whether true or false, your subconscious, being amenable to suggestion, will give the operator what seems to be a logical conclusion. In this instance, Mr. X suggested to his subconscious prior to the sleep state, "I do not believe. I do not believe in reincarnation. I will give no response." His subconscious mind accepted the dominant suggestion, which was that of Mr. X. Remember, your subconscious mind accepts the dominant of two ideas. Mr. X neutralized the suggestion of the operator, and you can see the humor of the response by Mr. X to the third question of the psychologist.

An Experiment with Mr. X's Sister

Mr. X's sister gave no contrary suggestion to her subconscious prior to the trance state, and the psychologist regressed her into different periods of history. She claimed to be Joan of Arc and spoke French in the trance state. At another time she was a princess in Egypt and launched out into a religious disquisition of religious beliefs in Egypt. She claimed that the pyramids were built by men who went into a semi-trance and lifted all the stones by the power of mind, cut them, and fitted them into place; that all this was accomplished without the sound of hammers or other metal tools; that mind did all these things.

There was, of course, no way of proving that she was a princess or Joan of Arc. After talking to her, I learned she had studied French for four years and had also lived in France. Furthermore, she also had visited Egypt and had studied the pyramids and Egyptian history. In the trance state, her subconscious mind, in response to the suggestion by the operator, dramatized a sort of composite of what she had read and studied. It could be called a fictionalized presentation, and her conclusions were syllogistically correct; that is, they were logically deducible from the premise of the psychologist that she had lived before and would tell us about it.

She accepted this suggestion, which became her major premise; whatever there was within the range of her own knowledge or experience, whatever she had seen, read, heard, or visited which tended to illustrate the idea in any way, was utilized by her subconscious. At the same time, her subconscious became totally oblivious to all facts or ideas which did not conform and which were not in accord with the operator's suggestion. Inductive reasoning is not a quality of the subconscious mind.

Have You Lived Before?

One of the most interesting factors discussed by many people is that they claim to remember their previous incarnations; furthermore, in remarkable detail some say they were priests in ancient temples, giving the period, location, and other interesting highlights. There is no doubt that some people seem to remember previous existences. They relate that the only way such memories can be explained is that they have actually lived before.

We are all immersed in a great pool of mind. Dr. Phineas Parkhurst Quimby said, "Our minds mingle like atmospheres." Your mind is a great reservoir containing the mental experiences and reactions of the ages. It is possible for a clairvoyant or other psychic to look back in time and see George Washington kneeling on the snow, but it does not mean that she is an incarnation of George Washington. It simply means that she tuned in on the mental picture or vibration, which is forever embodied in the universal screen of the universal subjective mind. All things co-exist in the mind-principle as an eternal now.

Important Points to Recall

Consider the fact that the sensory impressions of all men who ever lived are within you. You can easily tune in to the vibration of some previous experience which someone else had and think it is your own. The Life-Principle within you was never born and will never die. This Life-Principle in you, which is Infinite Spirit and Infinite Mind, has played all roles, created all countries, has been everywhere, has seen everything, and experienced all things. Think clearly and you will perceive through psychic perception that the One Mind operating through man wrote all Bibles and all books, and established all religions. That One Mind is within you, and this is why there are men and women not only in India and Tibet, but in other countries as well who do not have to travel to any part of the world to describe it in detail. Many clairvoyants are able to do this; yet the faculties of clairvoyance and clairaudience are within you and all men.

The Psychological Explanation of
Having Been There Before

Once I took a trip to Pondicherry in India. On arrival, I knew my way around. All the streets, buildings, and the market place were familiar to me. When I heard people speak, I said to myself, "I have heard these voices before." Let us look at this experience from the standpoint of the subconscious mind. Knowing that I was to visit Pondicherry, my subjective self traveled there while I was sound asleep. You could call this extrasensory travel, yet your subconscious is omnipresent, transcending time and space. While consciously asleep, I conversed mentally with many people, heard their responses and voices; furthermore, in that psychological journey, I saw all the beauties of the countryside.

I had been visualizing a wonderful trip, impressed this on my subconscious mind, and "went to sleep on it." My subconscious accepted the suggestion and dwelt there psychologically. When I consciously and objectively arrived there, I experienced all the subjective states. What I saw and heard objectively, I had seen and heard subjectively. Of course, I had heard that voice before and had seen that place before! The real truth is that no one, no matter who he is, can go any place, hear anything, or experience anything that does not already exist within him. Why is this? Because Infinite Mind is within him. Infinite Spirit or Infinite Mind does not have to travel, to learn anything, to experience anything, or to grow, expand, or contract. It is all there is. All things subsist now in the Infinite. It is the Ever-Living One, the All-Wise One, and the All-Knowing One.

Why You May Say, "It Seems I Have Always Known Him"

You may meet a man whom you are convinced you have always known. The reason is that he is an intimate of your mood. All tones are within you, just as countless notes and tones are in the piano; the tone you strike always was. When you say that you remember having lived in a certain city before and that everything seems familiar to you, it is quite possible that you had visited the place in the dream state, which you may have forgotten. But your subconscious or psychic mind forgets nothing; it registers and records all your experiences indelibly and infallibly. Your experience could also mean that you are awakening to that which was always known and which always existed within you. Remember, God—the Life-Principle—is within you. This Presence created all things. As you begin to awaken to the Divinity which shapes your ends, you will begin to realize that the whole world and all creation and experiences of the race are, therefore, within you.

Why Is It Possible to Remember Anything That Has Ever Transpired?

Of one thing you may be certain: It is possible to remember anything that has ever transpired on this planet. It is also possible to see what might happen in the future except it is changed through prayer. The real truth about you is this: The *I AM*-ness within you is your own consciousness or awareness. The Bible, in the Third Chapter of Exodus, called the name (nature) of God, *I AM*, which means Pure Being, Life, Spirit, Self-Originating Intelligence, Reality, or Pure Awareness. In other words, God indwells you, and when you say, "I AM," you are announcing the Presence of God within you

Therefore, when you do a little deep thinking, you will realize that the Infinite Spirit, or Infinite Mind within you, has been all men who ever lived, who live now, or whoever will live. This Mind-Principle within you has been Buddha, Jesus, Moses, Socrates, Lincoln, Shakespeare, etc. Your Awareness or Spirit has played all roles. It has been everywhere. It has seen everything. All is within It. Even the whole universe came out of your own I AM-ness.

The Infinite Mind operating in all men wrote all Bibles, spoke all languages, built all pyramids, wrote all books; therefore, you often read of many men throughout the world who, though poorly educated, but in a trance, state they speak 12 or 13 languages.

There Is Only One Being or Life-Principle

The One Being—faceless, formless, and timeless—individualizes in the form of man. All men are extensions of yourself, because there is only one mind. Each may condition it differently, but it is the one mind common to all individual men. The Life of you is One and Indivisible. It wears many garments. The word "humanity" means the One Being, limiting Himself by appearing as many and in human form.

Where Did You Come from Before You Were Born?

Always remember it is God coming into the world when a child is born. It is the Universal becoming the particular, or the Invisible becoming visible. You are the individualized expression of God. The Psalmist says, *It is He that hath made us* (Psalm 100). All of us have a common Father, a common Progenitor, the Life-Principle. It is called by many names; such as Allah, Brahma, Reality, Life, Being, Awareness, Consciousness, Living Spirit Almighty, and Self-Originating Spirit. The Bible tells you where you were before you appeared on this planet: *Thou hast been in Eden, the garden of God; every precious stone was thy covering* (Ezekiel 28:13).

Eden from a spiritual standpoint is a place of boundless bliss, indescribable beauty, and absolute peace. In other words, you came forth from God, the Boundless One, where you lived in fullness of joy, boundless love, all perfection, and harmony. These qualities of God are the precious stones which covered you. In other words, you were this Being living in the absolute state, and when your father and mother copulated and the ovum was fertilized, the Spirit entered in and was conditioned by the genetic record and the mood, mental attitude, and temperament of your parents. When you came forth, it was God being born and assuming the form of a child. The Bible says, *Before Abraham was, I am* (John 8:58). This means the same thing; i.e., before any manifestation or form appears, it first comes out of the invisible—the *I AM,* the Living Spirit Almighty.

Why Is an Innocent Child Born Deaf, Lame, Blind, or Crippled?

You might well ask why a healthy, vital, robust man becomes blind, deaf, tubercular, crippled with arthritis, or turns paranoiac or psychotic. The answer is: There is one universal law which cannot be broken. If the man hates the sight of someone, or if he is full of resentment, jealousy, vengeance, or hostility, all these generate destructive emotions which bring on all manner of functional impairments and diseases. There is not one law for a child and another for a man of 80 or 90. We are all under the same law as the child in the womb or the cradle. The Bible says: *Except ye repent, ye shall all likewise perish* (Luke 13:3). This means we are all immersed in the mass mind or the law of averages. Negative suggestions of the mass mind are continually impinging upon our mentality. Our mind receives according to our degree of receptivity. We can guard against negative circumstances through our psychic perception.

Reincarnation and Time Cycles

When a child is born, it is the Infinite Spirit assuming the form of that child. The personality—John or Mary—is the sum of the thoughts, feelings, and beliefs of each one of us. We tincture and color and modify the one Spirit by our beliefs, impressions, and conditioning.

Let us say that John, who lived in New York, passed on to the next dimension; the quality which was John lives in all beings throughout the world. Now, during a copulative act in some part of the globe, the tone or quality that was John is struck; this could be in China or Japan or elsewhere, and that quality or mood of the Infinite comes forth. It is not the personality we knew as John coming back; it is the tone of the Infinite coming forth.

The same instant that John died, instantaneously the same vibration could come forth in a member of another race and country. Cycles of 500, 600, and 1,000 years have nothing to do with this law. The Life-Principle is timeless; all tones are in the One. When you play on the grand piano, it will respond according to the notes you strike.

Man is the measurer, and... *with what measure ye mete, it shall be measured to you again* (Matthew 7:2). *For whatsoever a man soweth, that shall he also reap* (Galatians 6:7). You sow the seed in mind, and you reap the fruit of the seed; it will be the exact likeness of the seed sown.

It is definitely wrong to believe that you or anybody else is suffering because of the errors made in "past reincarnations."

You Are What You Think All Day Long

If you do not think for yourself, and if you do not cleanse your mind, you will suffer, because you have allowed fear, false beliefs, and erroneous concepts of the world to impinge themselves upon you. Then you are allowing the world-mind to do your thinking for you, thereby bringing about accidents, sickness, sufferings, and tragedies of all kinds. The mass mind or the world-mind is the mind which believes in disease, sickness, misfortune, accidents, and super-stitious beliefs of all kinds, hence the importance of cleansing our minds and keeping prayed up. There is no chance or accident, for all is law. There is a state of mind, a mental attitude, which is the cause of all.

You Are Here to Learn the Laws of Life

Suppose you put your hand on a naked electric wire. You would get burned or electrocuted. Why blame the law of electricity? Learn how the principle of electricity works and you can use it to bless yourself and others. The burn or the hurt you received was due to misuse or ignorance of the law. It would be foolish to say God was punishing you or that it was due to your karma (sins of a former life).

Suppose you jumped into the ocean and did not know how to swim. You would drown. You would not attribute it to a vindictive deity who is punishing you; rather, it would be due to your lack of knowledge as to how to keep afloat. The waters will hold up a boat or any man who learns how to swim or navigate.

You can fall off a cliff because of carelessness in climbing or through paying no attention to the instructor who is teaching you how to climb the mountain. The law of gravity is impersonal, without rancor or vindictiveness.

Why Do Babies and Young Children Meet with Sickness, Accidents, and Tragedies?

It is true that very young children do not think or reason until they reach a certain age; they are at the mercy of the moods, feelings, and atmosphere of the parents. Dr. Phineas Parkhurst Quimby 100 years ago pointed out that young children are like a white tablet on which all members of the family and relatives write something. The child's mind is highly impressionable, and it cannot reject the negative suggestions, fears, and anxieties of the parents. Naturally, it is susceptible to this emotional accent and reacts accordingly. This is psychic transmission affecting lives of others.

Psychosomatic physicians and psychiatrists are all familiar with the fact that children, until they begin to reason for themselves and pray scientifically, grow in the image and likeness of the mental and emotional atmosphere of the home. A careful degree of psychic perception can control the children's beneficial development.

The Law of Mind Is Good and Very Good

The law of mind is always just and eminently fair. If you hold up a horrible painting in front of a mirror, it will reflect exactly the picture held before it. Your mind is a mirror for the king and the beggar, and it always reflects mathematically and accurately the contents of your mentality. This is why the law is called good and very good. The ancient Hebrews said that the law of the Lord is perfect. It plays no tricks upon you, and that is why when you think good, good follows. Accordingly, your psychic perception can control the physical manifestation of your thoughts.

She Said She Choked People in a Former Life

While I was talking with a woman in Las Vegas whom we will call Mrs. B., she revealed that she had been suffering from asthmatic attacks for ten years and was using medication and injections occasionally without adequate relief. She had a "life reading" by a woman in Reno, who regressed her back about 200 years, and in the trance state she told the operator that she had choked prisoners in China during a rebellion in the Canton Province.

The Explanation

I explained to her in terms of psychic perception that

the Spirit, or God, within her never punishes; that all judgment is given to the son, meaning her own mind; and that she was punishing herself due to her guilt complex. I also pointed out that the operator who regressed her in the hypnotic state was guilty of imaginative folderol, too absurd for words.

During the colloquy, she mentioned that her mother had died from an acute attack of asthma; and furthermore, she added that she was not on speaking terms with her mother at the time of the latter's transition. I said to her, "Your asthma is due to your deep-seated guilt and remorse over the way you treated your mother, and you took on all the symptoms of your mother's asthmatic attacks in order to punish yourself."

Mrs. B joined with me in prayer for her mother, and she released her mother, wishing for her love, light, truth, beauty, joy, and happiness. She poured out love and goodwill to her mother and forgave herself for thinking negatively and ceased all self-condemnation. She used the following Biblical verses with remarkable healing results in adjusting her sense of psychic perception:

> Come now, and let us reason together, saith the Lord: though your sins be as scarlet, they shall be white as snow; though they be red like crimson, they shall be as wool (Isaiah 1:18).

> And their sins and iniquities will I remember no more (Hebrews 10:17).

> For thou, Lord, art good, and ready to forgive; and plenteous in mercy unto all them that call upon thee (Psalm 86:5).

> He shall call upon me and I will answer him (Psalm 91:15).

I, even I, am he that blotteth out thy trangres-
sions for mine own sake, and will not remember
thy sins (Isaiah 43:25).

Mrs. B began to dwell on these age-old Biblical truths
and continued to pour out love on her mother. At the end of
a few weeks, the attacks ceased and she became free. Mrs. B
realizes now that there is no time or space in mind or Spirit,
and that the past is dead. Nothing matters but this moment.
As she changed her thoughts and kept them changed, the past
was forgotten and remembered no more.

Why Some Children Are Born Blind, Deaf, and Deformed and Others Are Born Healthy

This question was asked 2,000 years ago. *And his disci-*
ples asked him, saying, Master, who did sin, this man, or his
parents, that he was born blind? Jesus answered, Neither hath
this man sinned, nor his parents: but that the works of God
should be made manifest in him . . . And said unto him, Go,
wash in the pool of Siloam, (which is by interpretation,
Sent.) He went his way therefore, and washed, and came
seeing. (John 9:2, 3, 7).

The question asked Jesus implied that the disciples
believed that this man must have been a sinner in a former
life; this belief was a part of the tradition at that time and
had permeated much of the Eastern world. People also
believed that the sins of the parents were communicated to
the children. In other words, if a father were tubercular, his
children would be also; if the father or mother were lame, the
children would be, too. Jesus rejected completely both
theories or beliefs, and turned to the Spiritual Power; he
healed the man instantaneously. You should take particular
notice that Jesus completely ignored this statement, which is
the ideal way to treat a falsehood or fallacy.

What Is the Law of Averages?

All of us are born into the race mind, sometimes called the mass mind or the law of averages. We are subject to the beliefs, opinions, and conditioning of our parents and our environment. As we learn the laws of mind in psychic perception we rise above the mass mind and transcend environmental conditioning and limitation. Jesus did not say to the blind man, "You are a sinner. You sinned in a former life and you must expiate for it now." No, he turned to the God-Power and his conviction of the Infinite Healing Presence healed the blind man. God—the Absolute Being or Life-Principle—condemns or punishes no man. Though a man be a cripple, he can be healed; if he is deaf, he can be healed; he is not a victim of some karma, which is an Oriental belief that our limitations and handicaps at birth are due to sins committed in a former life, which is called our karmic debt, and that we are now expiating for these errors or crimes.

The Mystery of Child Prodigies

One thing you must remember is that everything that has ever happened to mankind as a whole is recorded in the collective subconscious or unconscious of the race. For example, the genetic history of all men and women who have ever lived is also registered in that universal subconscious mind. As an illustration, an English officer in the First World War was in charge of a Scottish battalion which had suffered severe reverses. Suddenly he said, "I had an intense urge to lead them, and I began to talk to them in their own Highland Gaelic tongue. I felt I was somebody else and on a different battlefield doing the same thing as I had done before." He checked later on his ancestry, and he discovered a great grandfather who was a Scots Highlander and a captain in a Scottish regiment.

Biologists and geneticists have a ready explanation for that. He was under great stress and anxiety and sought desperately the best way to kindle a fire in the battalion, and his subconscious triggered a sudden recall of a genetic memory with a past scene of a similar nature, which brought about the feeling that he had experienced the same situation before. The genetic record of the entire race is within us. Scientists tell us that the genes of three billion people on this planet would not even fill up a thimble.

Look Back at Your Ancestry

You were a boy who had a father, who was a boy who had a father, who was a boy who had a father. Keep on going back and you will realize the genetic record and experiences of the entire race are within you. Keep going back and you will arrive at the primordial cell from which all of us originated, and the primordial cell originated with God—the Father and Progenitor of all life on earth. We are all intimately related and actually we are all brothers and sisters, having one common Father. This fact we can reasonably deal with through psychic perception.

A New Beginning Is a New End

In a lecture some time ago, I mentioned that I did not go along with the modern idea of reincarnation, which states that a person who is born deformed, crippled, blind, deaf, or with some other congenital defect has committed some crime or inflicted some injustice on others in a former life; that karmic punishment accounts for his imperfect condition—i.e., he is paying the penalty for his sinful acts in an earlier existence; that he must come back again and again until he makes atonement or Divine adjustment, and then he will be freed from the so-called wheel of karma.

All this does not hold water when you realize that no matter what your condition or circumstances are, when you begin to fill your subconscious mind with life-giving patterns and align yourself mentally with the Infinite Love, Infinite

Life, and Infinite Healing Presence, the negative patterns of your subconscious are obliterated and the past is forgotten and remembered no more. All this can be done with psychic perception. A new beginning is a new end, for the beginning and the end are the same.

Your Genetic Record

A woman who thought her child was a reincarnation of Paderewski began to realize that while she and her husband and the grandparents of the boy had no musical talent of any kind and were not particularly interested in music, the boy's great grandfather had been a musician in Hungary. It is reasonable to assume that the boy (their son) was born with the genes and genetic memories of his great grandfather, which were dominant, rather than those of his parents.

I explained to this woman that there could be five members of a family and one member may be entirely different in every way from that of his parents, brothers, or sisters. He is as far apart as the poles. This is explained by biologists as biological mutation, which is a basic alteration in his chromosome structure. The precocious child may also have clairvoyant and clairaudient faculties functioning, which are inherent in all people. It is also quite possible that the unusually gifted child received the musical talents and qualities latent in his ancestral stream.

What Is Biological Atavism?

The dictionary defines it as follows: "The reappearance in an individual of characteristics of some remote ancestor that have been absent in intervening generations." For example, Mozart composed music at five years of age. Before he was consciously aware of the laws of harmony, his subliminal or subjective mind knew them; this is true, also, of all men everywhere if we would awaken to the great powers within us.

Archbishop Whately, who was a mathematical prodigy, said that as soon as his conscious mind was exercised and educated, his faculty vanished. He had lost his gift of psychic perception.

What Is a Genius?

A genius is a man *en rapport* with his subconscious or psychic mind. It was through the subconscious that Shakespeare perceived great truths hidden from the conscious mind of man. Raphael, in his meditative moods, was in tune with the psychic powers of his subconscious, enabling him to draw forth the masterpieces which he called the Madonnas. Beethoven heard his music in the silence of his soul through his psychic perception.

Why Do Infant Mathematical Prodigies Lose Their Gift?

The child is in tune with the subjective mind; the subjective mind is amenable to suggestion, and an ordinary education teaches children to ignore the voice of intuition or clairvoyance and clairaudience. Instead of being taught to draw out the wisdom of psychic perception within, the latter is usually neglected, and the faculty atrophies and disappears. It could be preserved in the child by having the teacher impress the child's mind with the fact that he could always possess the mathematical psychic gift; that he would grow and expand as he learned the objective rules, figures, numeration, etc. The subjective mind of the child, being amenable to suggestion would retain his faculties of psychic perception, for "according to his beliefs" and those of his teacher, "would it be done unto him."

Some Remarkable Cases

Ralph Waldo Emerson was studying the classics before

the children in his neighborhood had learned to read. There is
nothing mysterious or supernatural about that. His ancestors
were spiritually oriented and lovers of psychic knowledge.
Undoubtedly, the mood of his parents at the moment of
conception influenced and brought about the proper genetic
influence also.

John Stuart Mill learned Greek at three years of age, and
at the age of seven had read Plato in the original, as well as
the works of Gibbon and Hume.

My father, who was a principal of a school in the south
of Ireland, was amazed at a boy of 12 who immediately
understood any mathematical problem or algebraic equation.
He could see through the most abstruse problem of mathematics and tell the answer without writing down a single
figure. My father recommended him to the local Bishop, who
saw that he was educated in the Seminary. He subsequently
became a Jesuit priest, and is now teaching mathematics in
the Far East. Looking back now, I am convinced the boy was
clairvoyant.

Realize a Great Truth

Anything any man has done, any other man can do.
God is within all men, and God is indivisible; therefore, all
that is necessary is for man to awaken to and mentally
accept completely these limitless psychic powers within him.

Your Storehouse of Memory

Your subconscious mind is a storehouse of memory, and
can be used to furnish you with any date or information you
have ever read. Solomon, a Lithuanian Rabbi, had such a
remarkable memory that he never forgot what he read. He
knew the Bible and the Talmud by heart, and he could quote
easily any passage requested. What he did, you can do. This is
fundamental and axiomatic through psychic awareness or
perception.

Many of you are familiar with the writings of Edgar Cayce. I heard him lecture a few times and was very much impressed by his sincerity and simplicity. He could memorize the contents of a book without ever looking at it. Your psychic perception can see without human eyes. Cayce was certainly clairvoyant and clairaudient. These faculties are in all of us, even though they may be dormant. We can develop them and quicken them. This has nothing to do with being born again and again in physical bodies. We do not grow or awaken in sidereal time and space. We must ascend the perpendicular beam within us, go up the hill of God where dwells the Living Spirit, timeless, spaceless, and ageless, where all things are known—the presence of God within us.

Edgar Cayce had very little ordinary school education. Tuning in on the subconscious mind in a sleep or trance state, he was able to diagnose the ills of patients in any part of the world; he was able to prescribe medicines and describe anatomical lesions, even though he knew nothing about materia medica, pharmacology, or the practice of medicine. He simply tapped the universal subconscious or psychic mind, and according to his belief was it done unto him. All the healings that followed were based on belief.

He was also able to place a book under his pillow and recite the contents verbatim. It is said that he could speak over a dozen languages in the trance state. After all is said and done, all languages ever spoken are in your subconscious mind, because you are one with the universal subconscious or unconscious. Undoubtedly, Edgar Cayce was also clair-audient, and he could have tuned in with doctors in the next dimension of life or extracted all his answers from the universal subconscious. He could have heard the voices or words of surgeons, osteopaths, and pharmacologists in the next dimension which no one else heard. His faculty of psychic awareness or perception was the foundation of his great powers.

Why Is There Inequality at Birth?

Frequently I receive letters saying, "Why is it some are born so poor and others are born into the lap of luxury? Some children are terribly handicapped and others not?" Many people are confused as to the meaning of *rich* and *poor*. Many people are poor in love, joy, faith, confidence laughter, and goodwill. Riches are of the mind. You are rich when you know you can tap the intelligence and wisdom of your subconscious psychic mind and bring your desires to pass. You are rich when your mind is full of peace, joy, love, confidence, and faith in the goodness of God in the land of the living.

Let us look at the case of Helen Keller. To say that her birth was an injustice or that she was being punished for a foul deed she had perpetrated on someone in a former life is wholly irrational, illogical, and most unscientific. Some say it was an injustice, because she was deprived of her sense of sight and hearing in infancy. She had a nurse, however, who used love and discipline, and Helen began to use the riches of her mind. Her eyes were enabled to "see" probably better than most people the color of all the pageantry in the opera; her deaf ears, in a similar manner, could "hear" the crescendos, diminuendos, and the full volume of orchestral music. She was aware of the clear notes of the lyric soprano. This is psychic perception.

History reveals the countless others who had all manner of afflictions, physical defects, and financial handicaps, yet they accomplished outstanding achievements in science, art, music, industry, and religion. Think about the countless numbers of people born into the lap of luxury, perfect specimens of humanity, many born with the proverbial golden spoon in their mouths. Ask yourself if they have accomplished as much good or have risen to such greatness as did those we mentioned who were born with poverty, illness, deformity, and all manner of handicaps

Would you insist that all these men and women whom I have mentioned must return again and again in order to receive justice? E. Henley, tortured by pain and a lingering sickness, said: " . . . I thank whatever gods may be for my unconquerable soul." Your soul is Spirit, and Spirit is God. In reality you are invulnerable and invincible. You are God walking the earth if you but exercise your psychic gift of perception.

How Some Look at Justice

There are many people who believe that because a man is born into vast riches, he will have to return here again on earth born into poverty to equalize things or to bring justice. Here they are talking about money, wealth, holdings, earthly possessions, etc. Justice is equitableness, righteousness, making things balance. The law is always eminently fair and just. "As a man soweth so shall he reap." This operates in the next dimension of life as well as here. However, you must perceive it through your psychic senses.

Reincarnation is not the answer to these questions. That would be very shallow thinking. You must not look at externals such as man's body, his environment, his parents, their wealth, their power or assets. Suppose a boy is born in Buckingham Palace with all the luxury, riches, and regal pomp surrounding him. So what? You are simply talking about externalities and not talking about the real boy who is a mental and spiritual being, who possesses the Kingdom of God within him. He will be rich or poor depending on how he uses the gift of God within him. As he sows so shall he reap, whether in this three-dimensional life or the next, which is the fourth dimension, which interpenetrates this plane and is all around us.

You Are Not a Victim of Karma

From the standpoint of Hinduism and Buddhism, karma

means action, seen as bringing upon oneself inevitable results, good or bad, either in this life or in a reincarnation. In theory, it is the cosmic principle according to which each person is rewarded or punished in one incarnation according to his deeds in a previous incarnation. The word *ka* means *to do, make;* and *ma* is *action of, result of.*

Our Bible says, *Whatsoever a man soweth, so that shall he also reap* (Galatians 6:7). You are not a victim of the past, for the simple reason that you can change the present, and your future will be your present conviction made manifest. God, the living spirit in you, is timeless and spaceless; therefore, a new beginning is a new end. When you pray scientifically, you are not dealing with time and space theories.

The man we call a murderer, thief, or a person of ill repute could, if he desired, become transformed in the twinkling of an eye. This could be accomplished by a great rise in consciousness, accompanied by an intense desire for God's love and peace.

How to Accept Your Good Now

Dwell on these wonderful words: *But if the wicked will turn from all his sins that he hath committed, and keep all my statutes, and do that which is lawful and right . . . all his transgressions that he hath committed, they shall not be mentioned unto him: in his righteousness that he hath done he shall live* (Ezekiel 18:21-22).

You are told in these verses that if a man will forsake the past and begin to practice right thinking, right feeling, and right action, he will transform himself. A new beginning is a new end. Get a new concept of yourself and walk forward into a new life through psychic perception.

Your Time Is Now

The *time* of which the average man speaks means his

relationship to earth in its orbital motion, and the position of the sun; it means his relationship to the events of today and tomorrow. Einstein said that if a man is talking to a beautiful, charming woman, an hour seems like a minute, and if he sits on a hot stove, 30 seconds seems like an hour, indicating that time in your mind is your thought, your feeling, a state of mind.

The ideal of your heart exists now. It is a concrete, living reality in the next dimension of mind. That book or play you plan to write is already in your mind. Affirm, "I accept the fulfillment of my desire completely now, and I rest in the conviction that my subconscious will bring it to pass." Remain faithful and you will experience the joy of the answered prayer. This is the psychic and perceptive approach.

The Author's View of Reincarnation

The time has come for scientific thinkers to make a clear-cut decision as to what to do with the millstone labelled "Reincarnation," which is discovered hanging from both Oriental and Occidental necks.

The theory of reincarnation is melioristic; that is, man is becoming better by the slow, exoteric process of putting on and off different habiliments of flesh and emotions. A man can come back a thousand times through wombs of various mothers, but growth and illumination do not take place in time or space. Growth and illumination take place by the transformation of the mind in tune with the Infinite, which is timeless and spaceless, and where all good subsists now. Accept the challenge: "Be ye transformed by the renewal of your mind."

We must not capitulate to a racial error perpetuated by the pronouncements of Eastern creeds and dogmas. Einstein has toppled the false gods of time and space. Today we know that spirit and matter are one. The scientific, mental thinkers look at the theory of reincarnation from a new standpoint altogether. They start with "the pattern on the Mount," wherein man is one with God.

We must cease building an edifice based on a slow-paced dream wherein millions of human beings—east and west—have been laid in the procrustean bed of karma and reincarnation to arise retailored in garments ill-befitting an invited guest to all the treasures of life within him. By believing in the theory of reincarnation, or countless cycles of carnal rebirths, you are drifting from safe mooring and placing bondage, restriction, and thralldom on yourself, for it is done unto you as you believe.

Let us have a declaration of emancipation from all the limited traditions and false beliefs of man—no matter how time-honored on Oriental altars. Let us cleanse our minds of all karmic, purgational fires by true faith and conviction of God's love and healing presence now, instantly available; and let us press on to the virgin fields of wisdom, truth, and beauty. We must not be deterred by a mirage of mere meliorism. All unworthy concepts must go into the limbo of spiritual ignorance; foremost among these stand this theory of reincarnation, whereby progress is decreed by age-old, earthbound thinking.

Jesus said: *The kingdom of God cometh not with observation. Neither shall they say, Lo here! or lo there!* (Luke 17:20, 21). The kingdom of life, love, truth, beauty, and all the powers of the God-head are within you now. When he declared: *Behold, now is the accepted time* (II Cor. 6:2). *Believe that ye receive them and ye shall have them* (Mark 11:24). *Before Abraham was, I am* (John 8:58). Was he not collapsing time and space relative to redeeming man from the thralldom of erroneous Oriental and Occidental beliefs?

Free yourself mentally from the belief in self-imposed fleshly, psychologically imprisoning embodiments. The "sons of God" must "leap for joy" beneath "the morning stars" of light, love, truth and beauty, which light up the heavens of your mind.

Karma, or reaping what you have sown, turns out to be inexorable only as long as you do not pray or meditate on the truths of God. As soon as you pray, you rise above karma, and the unpleasant consequences of past mistakes begin to be wiped out. No matter how awful the crime—be it murder or any other heinous offense—it can be expunged from the mind together with all the punishment that would ordinarily follow. Perfunctory prayer will not change matters. A deep hunger and thirst for God's love and grace, plus an intense desire to transform, are essential to wipe out the punishment that must otherwise follow negative and destructive thinking.

God's love passes all understanding, and it does illumine the path we tread. The wonders and blessings of God know no ending. Your journey is ever onward, upward, and Godward. You go from glory to glory, from mansion to mansion in our Father's house of many mansions. Life is progression. You are on an endless journey. Rejoice in your journey back to the One, the Beautiful, and the Good; there is no place else to go. It is the flight of the Alone to the Alone.

With a new vision, religion and science may both understand the mystic overtones of this ancient Hebrew meditation by affirming and believing the following:

Of all existence I am the source
The continuation and the end.
I am the germ;
I am the growth;
I am the decay.
All things and creatures I send forth;
I support them while they yet stand without;
And when the dream of separation ends,
I cause their return unto myself.

I am the Life,
And the wheel of the Law,
And the way that leadeth to the Beyond.
There is none else.

As you sharpen your focus of psychic perception as given you in this book, you will be organizing the full forces of your mind to achieve what you desire.

POINTS TO REMEMBER

1. There is one mind common to all individual men. A complete memory of all the experiences of the race is within the universal subconscious and may be tapped by you when you are *en rapport* with it through psychic perception.

2. Your subconscious mind does not reason inductively or argue controversially with you. It reasons deductively only and brings your premise (true or false) to what seems to be a logical conclusion based on the nature of the suggestion you give it.

3. In the hypnotic state, you will usually give the operator what he wants; i.e., if he believes that you have lived before and makes that suggestion to you, your subconscious will respond accordingly and weave a mosaic of fantasy and make-believe which is impossible to verify objectively.

4. If you give your subconscious mind a powerful suggestion prior to hypnosis that you do not believe and that you will not respond, and if your suggestion is more powerful than that of the hypnotist, he will not get results. Your subconscious accepts the dominant of two ideas.

5. Regression into past lives through hypnotic experiments results in a fictionized dramatization based on what you have read, heard, and experienced. Your subconscious is a master weaver and will

invent a sort of composite story or picture correlating with the nature of the suggestion given it in the trance state.

6. Your subconscious mind contains mental experiences and reactions of the ages. It is possible for a true clairvoyant to look back in time and see George Washington kneeling at Valley Forge. She could tune in on the mental vibration or mental picture in the universal screen of the subconscious. It does not mean that she had actually been George Washington at one time.

7. You can easily tune in on the vibration of some previous experience which someone else has had and think it to be your own. The faculties of clairvoyance and clairaudience are in all of us even though dormant. They can be awakened with psychic perception.

8. It is possible for you while sound asleep to dwell psychologically in the city or place you wish or intend to visit; and then when you go there objectively, you see, hear, and experience what you did subjectively. Therefore, you may think you were there before or you have seen that place before, etc. This is a very common experience. Today this is called extrasensory travel, which you may have consciously forgotten about.

9. In traveling, you may meet someone you think you have always known. He or she is simply an intimate of your mood. Our moods have their affinities.

10. Remember, Infinite Spirit, Infinite Mind, or whatever men call God, the Living Spirit, is within you and is operating through man and can be perceived psychically. It has created all things of Itself and also by means of man, for man is God in expression. This Infinite Mind has experienced all things,

knows all and sees all, and as you tune in with the Infinite, you will gradually awaken, using psychic perception, to the wonders and glories within you.